Endorsements

'In my most recent book, *By Your Side*, I have written about being aware of how loved family and friends stay connected to our lives, and all you have to do is be open enough to see the signs.

'In this book, Jacky and Madeline demonstrate, through personal experience, everything I have ever told people. I highly recommend this heart-warming book by two devoted daughters who sought the evidence that a loved one really was "always by their side"'

Colin Fry, psychic medium and life counsellor

'*Call Me When You Get to Heaven* is an inspiring and heartfelt read'

Rustie Lee, celebrity chef

'Isn't it reassuring to know each of us is being looked upon, even from way up in our big blue sky?'

Melissa Porter, TV presenter ... and Mummy

Call Me When You
Get to Heaven

Call Me When You Get to Heaven

Our Amazing True Story of Messages from the Other Side

Jacky Newcomb and Madeline Richardson

piatkus

PIATKUS

First published in Great Britain in 2011 by Piatkus

A CIP catalogue record for this book
is available from the British Library.

ISBN 978-0-7499-5661-5

Typeset in Palatino by M Rules
Printed and bound in Great Britain by
Clays Ltd, St Ives plc

Papers used by Piatkus are from well-managed forests
and other responsible sources.

MIX
Paper from
responsible sources
FSC® C104740

Piatkus
An imprint of
Little, Brown Book Group
100 Victoria Embankment
London EC4Y 0DY

An Hachette UK Company
www.hachette.co.uk

www.piatkus.co.uk

Dedicated to
Ronald Gerald Hill
17 September 1930–25 February 2008

In Heaven
In heaven . . . I can walk
In heaven . . . I can fly
In heaven . . . I can take my rod
To the carp lake in the sky

In heaven . . . I can eat
And sugar's not a treat
In heaven . . . I can stay up late
Steady on my feet

In heaven . . . I can dance
In heaven . . . I can talk
In heaven . . . I can drive my car
. . . I promise that I won't go far

Written and read by Jacky Newcomb
at the funeral of her father Ron

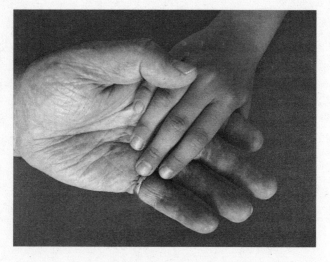

Ron's hand holding that of his grandson, James

(Photo by Nick Richardson)

Contents

Part III: Dad Had Died ... but He Certainly Wasn't Dead

Acknowledgements

Special thanks go to the many family and friends who were kind enough to allow us to use their stories here, and to all the people who were a part of Dad's life, both in heaven and on Earth.

Particular thanks to the living: Mum, Debbie, Di, John, Nick, Dave, Neil, Charlotte, Jasmine, Georgina, Jacob, Sam, Jim, Kyle and Rob. Also, to Sally, John and Daphne, John and Terry.

Of course, it goes without saying that the book wouldn't be the same without help and support from the other side, from Eric, Erne, Jack, Pat and Terry J. and our grandmother (Minnie), as well as several other deceased loved ones.

Last but not least, to Dad ... without whom this book would not have been possible. Thank you for keeping your promise Dad, and for calling when you got to heaven!

Prologue

Our dear and darling dad, Ronald Gerald Hill, died in 2008, aged seventy-seven. In the days that followed, we found mountains of photographs showing him laughing and giggling ... not just having fun, but enjoying the side-splitting kind of zest for life that characterised this wonderful man's entire existence.

Our father was an old-fashioned gentleman; a man who could envelop you in a giant bear hug of love. He'd soothe away all your troubles with a single cheeky smile that let you know everything was going to be all right ... and it always was.

He was kind, gentle, sensitive and adorable and made friends wherever he went. Everyone loved Ron, always happy, always smiling and always at the ready with his characteristic thumbs-up 'You OK?/I'm OK' gesture.

Ron had big feet and a 'handsome' nose. We joked about his large elephant ears, but he took it all with the greatest of humour. Usually sharp-looking in his everyday clothes, Dad also did a great line in cardigans – those terribly old-fashioned beige knitted ones with brown leather patches on the elbows. We all hated those bobbled cardigans, but after Dad died we realised that several of us had, at one time or another, buried our faces in them and that they were so evocative of him. Those cardigans *were* Dad; old, but comfortable and smelling sweetly of aftershave.

It was hard to believe that there would be no more cuddles, no more adorable grins and no more 'All right my darlings?', which was his favourite phrase to his beloved children and grandchildren. Dad was gone.

This is our story of Dad's life – and afterlife. It is a story told through the eyes of two sisters: two stories, two experiences, so two voices – Jacky's and Madeline's – and, just as he'd promised, Dad spent the few months after his death, letting us know that he'd made it safely to heaven.

Call Me When You Get to Heaven

Jacky: One of the things I remember most clearly about my childhood was standing at the top of the stairs when the police rang the doorbell. Dad had been in a serious car accident. It was a moment that set the scene for my life because Dad was always in hospital with one thing or another, and I was always worrying that he might die at any minute.

Maybe that's why I've devoted a large chunk of my adult life to studying the afterlife. I've spent hours poring over books about near-death experiences, and have been fascinated by stories of people who'd encountered angels and experienced afterlife phenomena. Do we really have guardian angels, I wondered, and, if so, where were Dad's angels when he was lying in hospital so often, sometimes at death's door? I was bitter, but my research helped me to put things in perspective.

By the time Dad was near to the end of his life I had written and published seven books on paranormal phenomena, mainly about people's life-saving and life-changing experiences with angels and the afterlife. Dad, who at first was slightly embarrassed by my work, became more interested when he discovered by chance that an elderly cousin of his had already bought and read my books; a close friend had also independently purchased a copy. His cousin was a fan without realising he was distantly related to the author! It gave Dad confidence that the subject matter was of genuine interest to people, rather than being perceived as weird.

When I first appeared on UK TV's *This Morning* back in April 2003, the subject matter had gone mainstream. The photograph taken of me with the presenters, Fern Britton and Phillip Schofield, was one of Dad's most prized possessions. Over the years, he acquired quite a collection as I met more and more well-known people in the course of my work. Dad had a little photograph album and carried it everywhere he went: as he walked around the local fishpond and stopped to talk to fishing friends, he'd inevitably pull out the album and brag about his daughter. Dad was (excuse the pun) hooked!

After that, he wanted copies of everything I did. 'Are you in any magazines this month?' or 'Do you have a copy of that piece about you in the newspaper?' he would ask. He kept a detailed file of everything; it was his boasting book.

Dad loved to tell people, 'My daughter goes on TV', but he was proud of all his daughters in different ways. He was a fan of us all, and when he was blessed with grandchildren he bragged about them too. He was very proud of his family and liked to keep us close.

Dad had a younger brother, Eric. After Eric passed away, the family had many paranormal experiences relating to his death. I always wondered if Dad would be able to communicate with the family from beyond the grave too. We were such a close family, and I knew the gap from losing Dad would never be filled, but if he were able to show us that he was still alive in some way it would help.

Dad had always promised to let us know that he'd made it safely to the 'spirit world'. 'Call me when you get to heaven Dad,' I'd say to him. 'Help me to write a book. Let me know that you arrive safely.' And sure enough, as we stood by his cold and lifeless body in the featureless hospital room, he gave us his first 'call' from the 'other side': two mobile phones rang with messages at the same moment – telephones which we'd switched off just twenty minutes earlier. How? Or maybe, who?

Numb with grief, but vaguely aware of the paranormal experience that had just occurred, we realised that Dad was in touch with us. He was trying to let us know that he had indeed made it to the other side of life, just as he'd promised. And this was to be the first of many such experiences.

Writing a book about them seemed like a good idea, it would certainly help with the grieving, giving us something to do. But it was only when we began collating the paranormal experiences that we realised quite how many there had been. And new stories were coming to us daily.

Madeline: I kept notes and records of Dad's many illnesses because when he was recovering, he always wanted to know what had happened to him. This was especially true when he had been in a coma. I wrote long descriptions about how it had felt for us, his family, during these worrying times and how these experiences brought us closer together. I let Dad read these stories when he was well, and he was impressed and fascinated by my accounts. He seemed excited that one day they might be published as a book.

I'd already been interested in psychic phenomena for over 13 years by 1999, and had done lots of research into these subjects. I visited mediums out of sheer curiosity, and practised self-hypnosis, using regression tapes, to experience my past lives. I read every book on the subject I could get my hands on, and went on to study regression and hypno-analysis. The secret, I found, was to remain open-minded to possibilities.

Jacky and I lived hundreds of miles apart, but whenever we got together we'd talk late into the night. On one such occasion, I told her I had written about Dad, and she advised me that, if I didn't finish the book while he was alive it would be an impossible task after he died; that I'd never cope emotionally. She was right!

On the night Dad passed over, Jacky was certain that she wanted to write about his life and afterlife because, as we talked about the phenomena that had already occurred, it was clear that a book was already emerging. However, she told me that she felt overwhelmed by the thought of writing it because of her immense grief. So it was a natural progression for both of us to tackle the book together, and we supported each other throughout this process.

Using my early stories as a starting point, complete with details and dates that might otherwise have been forgotten, we then started collecting other family stories, which came in thick and fast. We were amazed at the sheer number of paranormal events connected to Dad, which were being recounted to us by relations and friends, and we became excited, as the book seemed to be turning into something special.

Jacky and Madeline: So this is the story of Ron.

In Part One, we share the impact of what happened when he died and why we made the decision to write the book. Then, in Part Two, we go back to the beginning of Dad's life, his struggle for survival against the odds; and we take a look at the amazing and wonderful impression he made on all who knew him. Finally, in Part Three, we reveal his remarkable afterlife, because just as he'd agreed, he spent the next few months letting us know he'd made it safely to heaven. His visits from the other side made a massive difference to the way we grieved his loss, and we hope his messages touch you in the same way.

Call Me When You Get to Heaven

Introduction: A Psychic Family

> The most beautiful experience we can
> have is the mysterious.
>
> *Albert Einstein*

Jacky and Madeline: Paranormal phenomena and psychic abilities have appeared through many generations of our family – down both sides of the family tree, in fact.

Our Psychic Grandmother

When Mum was a girl her mother (our grandmother) had a recurring nightmare that her son Billy would drown. When Billy was staying in the Oxfordshire countryside with his uncle during the war, the dream was so real that our grandmother wrote to her brother-in-law, begging him to keep her ten-year-old son away from water. Then she wrote to her husband (our grandfather who was serving in the war), asking him to fetch Billy home. Reluctantly, Gramps agreed to collect Billy from his brother's house on his next leave of absence.

Tragically, Billy did go down to the river and was pushed in by older boys. He drowned, exactly as our grandmother had predicted, and rather than picking up his son as planned, Gramps arrived home in time to attend the inquest into his son's death.

Accident premonition

In later years, our grandmother had another remarkable premonition. She saw our grandfather wearing his army cap and greatcoat. In her vision, he was travelling in a vehicle which accidentally left the road. She saw the sunlight obscuring his view and glinting off the badge on his cap, just before he crashed. She worried about him all through the war, but he returned unscathed. He teased her gently because this time she'd been wrong. But she wasn't.

After our grandfather came home from the war, money was tight and he, like most young soldiers, continued to wear his heavy warm army coat and cap during the winter months. It was early one winter's day, and the low sun was glinting off the icy road when Gramps's van hit a pothole and left the road, throwing him clear of his vehicle, just as our grandmother had seen. Luckily, he lived to tell the tale, but he sustained a badly broken ankle and for ever after had to walk with a stick.

Because of the dramatic nature of these experiences, the details were often discussed in the family. However, Mum asked her mother *not* to share any premonitions she might have about *her*, just in case ... she didn't want to know! Our grandmother's abilities were fascinating, but not surprisingly, they could be frightening.

. . . and Psychic Uncles

Our great-uncle Erne (on Dad's side of the family) often talked about his Native American spirit guide. He believed this unseen spirit acted as a sort of guardian angel to him and his family, and he even hung a picture of a Native American over his bed.

Erne was our other grandmother's brother, born around the turn of the twentieth century, so he was clearly way ahead of his time. His daughter had multiple sclerosis and Erne learned the art of hands-on healing (spiritual healing) to try and ease her pain. There was no doubt about his ability to help; Dad's brother Eric (we'll hear more from him later) told us about visiting Erne for some healing on his arthritic hands. He said Erne's hands were red hot, as if he'd just lifted them off a radiator. Uncle Eric had no trouble with his arthritis for over a year after his healing session.

Spirit Relatives Visit After Death

Jacky: After Uncle Eric's death in 1991, family members would often dream about this funny and kind man. In these dreams, which seemed so real, he often passed on important messages, while during the day, every time his name was mentioned a light would flicker in the house or the doorbell would ring (no one was ever there – not a living person, anyway). I wrote about the family's experiences with Eric in several of my books and magazine columns.

Once, when I was talking to Dad about Eric's little 'jokes' from the 'other side', I quipped that he was probably listening in on our conversation at that very moment, and would no doubt let us know. I stood up and picked up my handbag ready to leave and, right on cue, the smoke alarm gave a single bleep in response. Both of us burst out laughing. This stuff was real and not frightening; it was funny – *Eric* was funny, that is, just as he had been in life.

Psychic Sisters

And so it was passed onto the next generation, Ron's four daughters are not immune to psychic phenomena either. As a child, I often woke up to see 'people' (or spirits) in my room and, later, had out-of-body experiences and predictions of my own.

One day, around the year 1990, when leaving the house for an overnight stay at a family friend, I had a premonition of a burglary. In my vision, I clearly saw someone entering the house and stealing the contents of my jewellery box. Rather than hiding my jewellery, as you might expect, I put on as many pieces of jewellery as I could wear in one go, deciding that the rest was part of a bigger 'universal plan' – fate, maybe.

As predicted, our home *was* burgled that night and all our gold was stolen. Distressing though this was, I decided *not* to replace the stolen pieces, but to use the insurance money for driving lessons instead (thereby changing my life for the better). My prediction, in this case, had turned out to be helpful, after all.

Our sister Debbie recalls out-of-body experiences too, and remembers waking on more than one occasion to find herself floating above her body. She has also heard warning premonition voices from several deceased relatives, as well as experiencing dream visitations. Their advice has always been helpful, even life saving.

Madeline: I have been researching the psychic and para-normal world for over twenty years. I've investigated past-life regression and had many experiences of my own, through dreams and hypnosis. My fascinating studies have taken me from an irrefutable belief in the afterlife to quantum physics and parallel universes – the science behind the mysteries. Yet the more I discover, the more questions I have!

Our youngest sister, Dianne, a natural medium from birth, now uses her abilities to help others. Psychic and predictive dreams are an everyday occurrence for her too.

Our children too have shown many instances of psychic insight. But more of this later . . .

PART I

Our Last Week with Dad

Chapter 1

And then there was light

Those who say it can't be done should not interrupt
the person doing it.

Ancient Chinese proverb

Out-of-body and Near-death Experiences

Jacky: 'Actually, there's something I've been meaning to tell
you,' Dad began. 'One night, when I was in hospital, I saw
death ...'

'What do you mean?' I asked, awestruck.

'Death and life are *this* close,' he went on, illustrating his
point with hands held closely together. 'Life and death are parallel, and you know – it's OK to die. Death is fine.' He grinned.

We were uneasy. Although all of us were familiar with spiritual experiences, this was something new to Dad, and it was a
little worrying that he was taking it all in his stride. Why was he
seeing death?

Dad had recently been released from hospital. He'd faced so

many illnesses and accidents throughout the years – there always seemed to be another hospital or another doctor's visit. This loving, sweet, kind and sensitive man had lived through hell, but always seemed to bounce right back.

His last hospital visit had knocked him about more than any other though. At seventy-seven years old, he seemed frail now – sad, tired; and we all sensed it.

It was February half term. Mum and Dad's bungalow was up for sale, and Mum was busy showing prospective buyers around their home. Madeline was visiting and had been helping to get the house ready to sell. She and Dad had been dispatched to my house around the corner, 'out of the way', until the viewing had taken place, giving us this rare opportunity for a spiritual discussion.

Madeline sat on the sofa clutching tightly on to his hand, as if letting go would mean so much more than simply unclasping it. They exchanged a loving smile.

Dad continued. 'I saw my granddad and two of my aunties. They were beckoning for me to go with them, but I wasn't ready.'

Wasn't ready? Wasn't ready to die – is that what he meant? We'd heard this before – the classic near-death experience (or NDE) – and knew it was real; relatives from heaven-side like to collect the dying, escorting them 'home'. Having studied hundreds and thousands of case histories in the course of researching my books, I knew that Dad had been given a choice to go to the other side, at the moment he spoke of, or to stay here on Earth a little while longer.

Madeline: Near-death experiences are usually reported either after an individual has been pronounced clinically dead or has otherwise been very close to death. NDEs are comparable to out-of-body experiences because of being outside of one's physical body, but are often, though not always, accompanied by other lucid experiences, including the classic 'tunnel' and powerful 'light', seeing deceased relatives or religious or spiritual beings and deciding, or being encouraged, to return to one's body, often reluctantly.

Improved cardiac-arrest survival rates mean that the number of reported NDEs is on the increase. Scientists often regard such incidents as hallucinatory, while paranormal experts and a number of mainstream scientists claim them to be evidence of an afterlife.

Jacky: Madeline and I exchanged glances. We both realised the significance of what Dad was saying. But we tried not to panic. Near-death experiences were often just that – *near* death, but not necessarily followed by death. Many people went on to live as long as seventy or eighty more years after such an experience.

Dad continued; he was on a roll now: 'Then I found myself floating out of my body, and I knew it was real. You girls have talked about these things for years; I've wanted to believe it was true and now I know it is.'

This was correct; we'd always talked about the paranormal. I recalled an experience from just a few days earlier that I'd spoken to Mum about at the time.

'I was sitting up in bed the other night, reading, and I swear someone came into my room,' I'd explained to Mum.

'Someone?' asked Mum.

'Spirit energy, something like that'

'What did John say? Did he feel it too?' Mum was intrigued.

'Well, John was still downstairs. I guess he'd fallen asleep in front of the TV.'

'Was it Eric?' asked Mum. Dad's brother was a regular spirit visitor. Many family members experienced visits from our dead uncle in dreams, so Mum certainly didn't think I was crazy for discussing such things.

'No – I'm used to Eric,' I continued, 'and I know it wasn't him. I wasn't frightened, but someone definitely came into my room.'

The experience had been a puzzle. However, now that we were sitting quietly with Dad, drinking tea in my small, modern living room, I had a feeling that the mystery was about to be solved. I was going to find out who my late-night mystery visitor had been.

'Then what happened?' we asked Dad, prompting him to continue with his story.

'Well, at first I was worried and didn't know what to do, so I decided to fly over to *your* house. Didn't you see me?' he asked me.

'When?'

'Last Friday.'

'No, really?'

'Yes, I flew out of the ward, down the corridor and out of the hospital. Then I flew down the dual carriageway, and all the way to your bedroom!'

'What? You literally "flew" as a spirit, using the same route you would have done if you'd been in a car?'

'Yes!' he said, excitedly. 'I saw you sat up in bed reading – but where was John?'

And then it dawned on me; the night Dad was talking about was the night I had felt someone in my room. It had been Dad who I'd 'felt', but couldn't see. Dad seemed disappointed.

'Couldn't you see me?' he pressed. 'I could see you so clearly!'

At this point I reassured him that everything he'd seen *was* exactly as it had been on that night. Dad was comforted. But I still teased him about it:

'You shouldn't enter a lady's boudoir without permission,' I joked.

'It felt so real,' Dad went on. 'It was just like you talk about in your books. I saw the world differently that night. You know I could see both sides of life, and with everything I've been through I know there are loads of people who are worse off than me . . . ' he trailed off.

Dad seemed elated. It was a spiritual breakthrough, an epiphany. But there was still more.

'I decided I could help people while I was out-of-body,' he said, earnestly.

'Like Uncle Eric?' we joked.

'Yes!'

Dad seemed to have reached a place where he could imagine living his future life as a Spirit. He could finally accept that he was more than 'just his body' – that in fact he didn't need his body at all.

Madeline: Being able to view people in another room, or observe objects that are impossible to see from the viewpoint of the individual having the experience, has been put forward as hard evidence of the soul physically leaving the body.

The Promise

Jacky: Our conversation with Dad that afternoon was totally riveting and we were all interested to know what he planned to do with his new-found out-of-body flying experiences. We joked about him helping us when he finally crossed over to the heavenly side himself.

Then, with a glint in his eye, Dad asked, 'Do you *pay* Eric to help you write books?' And we all burst out laughing. He loved his new experiences and was in awe of the whole thing.

'When you die and start to "work" with Eric full time, are you going to come back and help me write a book?' I asked cheekily.

'Of course, I will my darling,' he said, with his usual grin.

Then the telephone rang. It was Mum saying that the viewers had finished looking around the house and had loved it; it was now OK for Dad to come home.

We all felt a little disappointed at having to finish our amazing conversation.

A Strange Feeling

Madeline left Mum and Dad's home for her cottage in Cornwall that afternoon. I had to get my suitcase packed as John and I had planned to meet up with her again in a few days time for a short holiday, and I was more than ready for the break.

Dad was now at the stage where he had several hospital visits every week; different hospitals for different reasons. We had all taken turns driving him to appointments but we were getting behind with work. On the Monday before our holiday, Dad had to go into Derby hospital for the week. Mum had booked a taxi, a welcome relief, but late on Sunday night I had a strong urge to drive him personally. It was too late to ring and offer, but early the next morning I phoned the taxi company myself and cancelled their ride.

Mum was surprised when I telephoned. 'But the taxi is already booked,' she said.

'No, I'm going to take you. I had a strange feeling about it. I want to do it; anyway, I've cancelled the taxi now.'

When I arrived at the house half an hour later, Dad was standing at the door, smartly dressed as always. He looked strong and proud, but his eyes betrayed the pain he was suffering. I gave him a hug and he held me tightly. A strange feeling overwhelmed me at that moment: What if this is the last time I hug him, I thought. Was this why I'd felt the sudden need to drive? I held on to Dad, not wanting to let go; the hug stretched on and on, as I rested my head against his chest, breathing in his lovely aftershave.

Then Mum was ready to go, and all too soon we bustled into the car. Dad sat in the front seat. He was quiet, scared even. Mum and I chatted about anything and everything to try and lighten the mood, yet I felt near to tears for the whole journey.

Debbie was visiting Dad that evening, so when I dropped them off there was no need for me to stay, nothing for me to do. Dad picked up his stick, ready to go. I wanted to rush round and open the passenger door for him, but another car had pulled up behind me. I felt hurried and had to be ready to pull away. Mum got out of the car.

'Thanks for the lift,' she called out.

Dad was already walking away, preoccupied. For the first time ever, he never looked back, never said goodbye. My stomach lurched. I wanted to run after him, grab him, hug him and never let him go, but the driver in the car behind me was revving the engine impatiently, and I drove away crying, not really knowing why.

The Final Call

Madeline: My children had gone back to school after the half-term break, and we'd planned to grab a few days away with Jacky and John, my husband's parents having kindly agreed to look after the boys. We would have three days together – Tuesday, Wednesday and Thursday. I'd found somewhere in the Cotswolds, about halfway between our two homes, and booked a hotel there.

The weather was cold, but then, it was February, after all. The hotel was lovely, and we spent much of the time in the 'Red Room', a plush sitting room, furnished with leather armchairs, where we ordered tea and scones, and simply chatted. We had dinner out in the evenings, and went for little drives, exploring some of the area, but mostly we were just pleased to be in each other's company. Three hundred miles is a big distance between families, and although I knew I couldn't give up my beloved Cornwall, it was always nice to catch up with family, and something we tried to do fairly regularly.

Dad had gone into hospital the same week for a simple procedure. Jacky had dropped him in on the Monday morning, before setting off for our break early on Tuesday.

I'd visited Mum and Dad the previous week, to help get their bungalow ready for the sale. We'd cleared and sorted for three days, and it now looked fantastic, like a show home. Dad had been thrilled to receive an offer on the property the day I left. They could now look forward to moving into their exclusive retirement apartment together.

As I arrived home from our short break on the Thursday evening, the telephone rang. It was Dad. He was home from hospital.

'Hello, my darling.'

'Hi, Dad. How did you get on?'

'Fine, no problem at all.' He sounded delighted.

'Brilliant! Well done!' I enthused. 'Fantastic Dad, I'm so pleased for you.' I grinned into the telephone; it was lovely to hear him in such high spirits, as he'd been rather down following his last operation. This conversation turned out to be hugely significant to me, although at the time, I merely thought that perhaps life would settle down a little from now on. How wrong one can be.

Chapter 2

'I don't want you to worry, but...'

In this life we cannot do great things. We
can only do small things with great love.

Mother Teresa

I'll Hang On to His Watch ... For Now

Jacky: 'Now I don't want you to worry, but Dad is in hospital.
He's been sick all night and I called for an ambulance. I don't
want you all to rush in ...' As usual, Mum tried to hide the
concern in her voice.

'What happened? Where are you?'

'I'm at the hospital; I don't want you to worry.' There, she'd
said it again, her anxiety clear.

We'd returned home from our Cotswold break four nights
previously, and I hadn't been able to visit Dad since arriving
home as I'd caught a cold, and didn't want to pass it on. Now

Mum explained that Dad had been vomiting throughout Sunday night. She had tried to contact us, but kept getting the wrong number or the calls were missed. My daughter, Georgina, had heard the phone ring at around six in the morning, but had gone back to sleep. Finally, Mum had got to speak to me just before 9 a.m.

'Dad's in the observation ward,' she said.

'Right we're coming in, I'll meet you there.' It was a well-known pattern. Debbie, Dianne and I were local – we always rushed in; we always wanted to be with Dad and be at our mother's side. One day it would be the *last* visit, but we'd never know when that might be.

Mum relented and gave a few instructions for things she wanted us to pick up from their house on the way – his slippers, his glasses and his hearing aid. Before leaving, I sent John an email, to let him know what was happening. I tried to keep my tone light, hiding the turmoil I felt inside. We were all always frightened when Dad went into hospital.

I arrived at Mum and Dad's house and, as I walked into their bedroom, I spotted Dad's watch by the bedside. My stomach turned over as I reached out for it; I caressed it in my hands before putting the oversized band on my wrist. I'll just hang on to this ... for now, I thought, as if I had a feeling of what was to come. I wasn't going to let go of that watch.

I rang Debbie and Dianne. 'I'm going to the hospital now, Dad's been taken ill.'

They both responded saying, 'Pick us up', without hesitation. Dianne said she would bring water, orange juice and cereal bars – 'traditional' food for our long stays in the hospital waiting room.

We were more quiet than normal in the car, travelling the familiar route. We walked into the emergency waiting room before confidently strolling through to the observation area, not waiting to ask permission. No one challenged us. Confidence, along with familiarity does that.

'Could you show us where Mr Hill is please?' we asked. A nurse pointed to a curtained area. As we moved the curtain aside Dad spotted us and smiled with relief.

'My beautiful girls are here!' He grinned. He seemed thrilled to see us, as always.

I waved, but didn't approach the bed because of my head cold. The three days away with Madeline had been enormous fun, but the cold had sneaked up on me suddenly. I didn't need this now. I felt cross that I was ill, but didn't dare risk passing on my infection, although everything in my being made me want to rush over and hug my father. He looked shrunken and pale ... but nothing I hadn't seen on numerous occasions before. I tightened my silk scarf around my mouth and stayed back, as my sisters held his hand and gave him the hugs that I couldn't.

Mum looked tired too. She'd also been up all night. It's too much, I thought. We can't keep doing this any more. Dad can't keep doing this. I hate it. Why do we have to keep seeing someone we love suffer? Why couldn't he be well and at home with us?

The doctors took Dad to a different observation area. My sisters slipped away for a coffee and when they returned I took Mum for a break too.

Mother Teresa

Dad was chilly and Dianne went in search of an extra blanket, but all she could find was another sheet to wrap him in. Dad continued to shiver and, thinking of the heat he must be losing through the top of his balding head, Debbie unzipped the overnight bag they'd fetched from home and carefully draped a plush blue towel around his head.

Mum and I arrived back from our coffee and noted that Dad's eyes now appeared the colour of a pale blue sky – his normal clear hazel eye colour had disappeared, and the brightness of the towel around his head made him look ethereal somehow. Dianne whispered that he looked like Mother Teresa. Debbie laughed, then shared the joke with Dad, who laughed too. I could only smile. The short distance to Dad from the end of the bed where I sat, isolated by my own sickness, seemed enormous. How I longed to reach out to him, grateful now for the extended hug I'd had just one week earlier when I'd last seen him.

'What will you do if Uncle Eric comes for you?' Deb teased Dad. He knew exactly what she meant: if his deceased brother came to take him to the pearly gates.

'Tell him to bugger off!' was his reply, and we all giggled.

Mum noticed a spare pillow on an empty bed, and knowing Dad liked two, took it and lovingly plumped it up behind his shoulders. He had cramp in his feet, possibly from being dehydrated, so Mum massaged his ankles too, noting how uncommonly small and shrunken they looked in her hands.

'You're always looking after me,' Dad said, smiling at her gratefully. He had stopped shivering now; the intravenous painkillers were obviously working. But the doctors had warned us, his kidneys were failing.

'Are you warm enough now Dad?' Debbie asked. Dad snuggled his face into her open hand as a child might do. And, in a slight reversal of their daughter/father roles, she lightly cupped his cheek in a tender and affectionate way.

'Lovely!' he said with a grin.

We all said goodbye to Dad and told him we'd see him later. The plan was to have some soup down the pub, then return to hear the doctors' assessment of Dad's condition. It would give us time to chat and Dad time to sleep. It was clear he was exhausted and there was nothing more we could do to help. We left Mum sitting on the bed behind the dividing curtain for an extra couple of minutes, and lingered in the familiar waiting room.

Mum joined us presently, but then realised she'd forgotten something, and Debbie offered to go back. It crossed my mind that this might be the last time anyone would see Dad alive – I'm not sure why – and I wondered if I should take this opportunity to go back in. It pained me more than anything that *I* hadn't been able to stroke his cheek. But I knew I couldn't get too close to him. A cold could be fatal to someone as vulnerable as Dad was. I decided I wouldn't go back. And I was happy with the decision. I'd spent a lifetime with this gorgeous man, I reasoned, and had loved him every single day. I was satisfied that we'd had many wonderful moments together and that everything was as it should be. And anyway – we were only going for lunch and I'd be seeing him later. When *was* it OK to say goodbye, after all?

Debbie, making the last-minute return to Dad's bedside, told him that he was the best dad and granddad anyone could ever have; then she gave him an extra kiss and whispered, 'I love you, Daddy.'

Mum approached the doctors' station. 'How long will you be keeping Mr Hill in?' she enquired.

'If he stops being sick, he could come home in the morning,' she was told.

Satisfied, we walked down the corridor. Another hospital visit over with.

Happy to Leave Him

Madeline: Debbie rang me just after 9 a.m. on Monday morning. I was lying in bed, thinking about getting up and ready for my dental appointment.

'Dad's been taken into hospital by ambulance,' she told me. My stomach tightened, but I said nothing, waiting for her to continue. 'He was being sick in the night, apparently. Mum went in with him, and we're just on our way in. We don't know much, it could be a viral infection. I'll phone you when I know more.'

'Right. Thanks . . . ' I replaced the receiver. Should we travel up, I wondered. It was a five-hour journey. How poorly was he? I'd have to wait and see – perhaps I'd get the suitcase down and make a few arrangements, just in case. I telephoned my in-laws in the next village and asked if they'd be able to have the boys for us if we needed to make a sudden dash to the Midlands. 'Of course, no problem,' was their reassuring reply.

I quickly showered and dressed, and my husband and I made our way into town. I received a text message from Jacky saying, 'Think it might be a viral infection. Pack a bag, but don't rush up.'

Soon afterwards, another message came through: 'Could be gastroenteritis, sending him for tests.' I needed more information, and replied, saying: 'I don't know how to feel. Should I be worried?' Jacky said, 'Just leaving him now. He's tired, but don't feel he's dying at this moment! Happy to leave him . . . '

Jacky: The four of us felt lost, but continued on to the pub for lunch, as planned. It provided some normality in an otherwise stressful day. The soup was good and we spent the next hour laughing together about the towel wrapped around Dad's head. We planned who would make the evening visit, and then we all went home.

When the call came later, we were all caught by surprise.

Madeline: Mum rang me as soon as she got back from lunch. She sounded calm, but then she always did. She was so used to Dad's hospital visits; they were second nature now. She told me, 'He looked dehydrated, Madeline; he seemed to visibly shrink before my eyes.'

'Shall we come up, Mum?' I asked her. 'I've got a case down, ready.'

'There's no point. Let's just wait and see.'

Wait and see . . . It was always wait and see.

Within the hour, Mum was on the phone again.

'Madeline?' she half sobbed.

'Yes, Mum. What is it?'

'The hospital has telephoned. Dad's in a bad way; they've told me to come in straight away.'

'Oh God,' I said. 'OK.'

'I've got to go. I have to phone Jacky,' Mum managed. She had rung me first, perhaps because I was the last person she'd spoken to. I picked up the phone and dialled our sister Debbie to let her know. Then I threw some stuff into a suitcase for the boys to take to Grannie's, and some more stuff in another case for us. What would I need? How much should I take? I couldn't think straight.

Jacky: It was late afternoon when the hospital rang Mum.

'I think you should come in now, Mrs Hill. Mr Hill has taken a serious turn for the worse,' they explained.

As Mum rang to tell me the news she was crying. I knew it was serious – more so than before. I said I would collect her and jumped right back in the car. If it's bad news, I want to drive, I said to myself; I'm the eldest, I'm the strongest – I can do this. But he always recovers, why am I worried this time, I wondered.

I picked up Debbie and as we waited outside Mum's bungalow, I fiddled once again with the oversized watch, still on my wrist – so reminiscent of Dad's tanned arms, and a symbol of his strength.

The Disappearing Password

Having picked up Dianne, we quickly pulled up at the hospital and abandoned the car in a doctor's car park. As we headed quickly to the emergency room, my mobile began ringing. My daughter Charlotte was on the other end of the phone and she was worried. She *knew* something was wrong. She'd typed her usual password into the computer at home, but it wouldn't accept it. Her password, she informed me, was 'RONALD HILL', and she took its disappearance as a 'sign' from her Granddad. Why *had* 'RONALD HILL' gone from her computer? Was he dying? Was he dead? Was he trying to tell her something? I didn't know; I couldn't reassure her.

As we entered the hospital, we switched off our mobile phones. Nursing staff avoided meeting our gaze as we walked in, glancing at us sidelong, with a strange mixture of sympathy, sadness and fear.

What was happening? What was going on? We were about to find out.

Chapter 3

In my end is my beginning

I am Alpha and Omega, the first and the last.

King James Bible, Revelation 1:11

The Family is Here

Jacky: I could feel my heart beating loudly in my chest as we walked up to the nurses' station. Immediately, the ward sister walked over to us. She seemed to stumble over her words: 'Oh, the family are here ... would you like to wait in my office please? The doctor wants to talk to you.'

What? Why weren't we being shown in to see Dad? We all picked a seat, no one dared to speak; no one exchanged a glance. After ten minutes, the ward sister came back in.

'Have you seen the doctor yet?'

We all shook our heads.

'Has anyone told you how ill he was?' she began. *Was?* The nurse faltered, as we looked up expectantly. Then, instantly, she seemed to make a decision before walking over to her desk, then momentarily shuffling some papers before sitting down. She took a deep breath.

'I can't leave you waiting like this. It's not fair. I'm sorry . . .' she began. 'Mr Hill passed away.'

Someone shot me in the heart. I felt it, but there was no gun. The nurse's words were the bullet. Dad passed away. He's dead. He died. Did she say he died? Oh my God . . . he's dead.

The rest of her speech was a blur. I'm sure she told us when and how he died, but I missed it. I heard nothing after 'passed away'. The world around me became a slow-motion movie. Three small screams of pain and shock pierced the air, from Mum, Debbie and Dianne, but I was still calm, still frozen in shock.

'Can I borrow a phone please?' I asked, almost matter-of-fact, on autopilot now. Aware that Madeline was in Cornwall at this moment, awaiting news, I was now haunted by my final text to her: ' . . . I don't think he's dying yet'. How wrong I'd been. I wanted her to hear now whatever the nurse would say to us at the same time *we* heard it. I wanted her to *be* here, to be with us as a family.

'I need to ring Madeline,' I said. Then, I suddenly remembered: Is it my job to do this? Strangely, I became aware of protocol. Should her mother tell her? 'Does anyone else want to tell her?' I asked. But no one else could speak. It was just as I'd rehearsed many times in my mind. I'd somehow known that I would be the one to make this long-distance call. The call we never wanted to make.

'Yes, of course. Here you go,' said the nurse, handing over the phone. I placed it back on the desk, not trusting myself to hold it. Then I realised I couldn't remember my sister's telephone number. With heartbreaking sobs filling the room, like white noise on a radio, I looked helplessly around the room, seeing everyone's shocked faces. Someone has to function, I thought. Someone has to make the call. I am the eldest. It's my duty. It's my job. What's her number?

Debbie gathered herself together and immediately hurried over; she *could* remember Madeline's number. She wrote the number down, but even seeing it on paper in front of me, I was still unable to dial and my sister noticed.

'Shall I tap it in for you?'

'Yes, could you please?' I was relieved. Each of us was functioning as half a person with our grief, but together we were two halves of one whole. Both halves needed to complete the simple task.

I knew that Madeline and her husband were standing by in Cornwall, ready to make the three-hundred mile drive on our advice. I immediately felt guilty. Should I have rung sooner and told her to start driving? But of course, we didn't know.

I made the call I'd rehearsed silently a hundred times. My brother-in-law Nick answered the telephone, as I knew he would. I broke the news: 'I'm sorry, Dad didn't make it. He died,' I added, as if to emphasise the point.

I heard Nick's gasp of shock. 'Oh my God, no way. I can't believe it. Are you all OK?'

'Yes, we're fine.'

'Right, we're on our way. We'll get there as soon as we can.'

'OK, Nick. Drive carefully. I'll see you later.'

Our darling Dad, Ron Hill passed away aged seventy-seven, after a lifetime of illness. Ironically, when the final moment came we were totally caught off guard. All those hours sitting by his bedside, and still he died alone, while his family were eating soup.

Yet had some part of me known? Had I really *not* seen it

coming? I recalled my last-minute cancellation of his taxi, so I could take him to the hospital just a week before – that final time. And the last time I'd hugged him; that moment when I couldn't let go. Was a higher power letting me know, preparing me, giving me one last chance to say goodbye? Then that feeling as I'd put on his watch – the watch I never gave him . . . the watch that was still on my wrist.

Shock

Madeline: I heard the telephone ring, and made my way into the lounge. My husband, Nick, had already answered and was deep in conversation; I tried to get him to look at me, I wanted to know the information he was hearing, but he remained shuttered, his eyes turned away, concentrating on the latest news about Dad.

'Oh my God . . . I can't believe it. Are you all OK? Right, we're on our way. We'll get there as soon as we can.'

What was the news? How was he?

Nick hung up the phone, finally looking me in the eye. 'I'm so sorry; your dad didn't make it.'

'What?'

'I'm so sorry. He died.' Nick's face crumpled, as he reached to pull me into his arms.

I remained rigid. This wasn't true. I'd been waiting for an update – to know if he was better or worse. Not this . . . no.

'NO. No . . .' I covered my face and howled in disbelief. Dad always pulled through; how could he be dead? I pulled away and went to sit on the edge of the sofa.

'I'm so sorry . . .' Nick followed me, laying his hand on my back as I sobbed. When was the last time I spoke to him?

What did I say? It was our telephone conversation on Thursday night. I was pleased for him, enthusiastic at his news: 'Well done Dad! Brilliant!' It was a good last conversation – the last time I'd spoken to him; the last time ever now.

We'd known when I heard that Dad had taken a turn for the worse that we would have to make the journey to the Midlands. We'd actually just settled the boys into the car, ready to take them to my in-laws, when the telephone rang.

Nick now fetched the boys back in and, as they stood in the conservatory at the front of the house, he broke the devastating news to them. Jim cried immediately, but Sam, the eldest, just stood in stunned shock, unable to speak properly. He opened his mouth but no words came out.

The boys then ran into the lounge and we fell into a tight hug, all of us together. As we broke apart, Jim stayed close still crying. We talked with them for nearly an hour, and explained that Granddad had gone to a better place, where he would be free from pain and any more operations. He would still be around us, we told them; we just wouldn't be able to see him any more. Sam still couldn't speak, but nodded his agreement. Jim wanted to know more about heaven.

Talking about our beliefs was reassuring for all of us. It reminded me that death wasn't the end. Dad *would* still be around, I was still deeply shocked, but talking death through with the boys was calming and brought *me* some clarity.

Nick then rang his parents, breaking the news about Dad, telling them we still wanted to bring the boys round so we could leave straight away.

The First Sign

Jacky: I put the phone down and the nurse asked if we still wanted to talk to the doctor. 'No,' I said, making the decision for everyone and shaking my head. It's too late now, I thought. Nothing anyone can say will bring him back. It didn't matter what the doctor had to say, I didn't want to know. But I needed to see Dad – to see for myself that he'd died.

'I want to see him. Can we see him? Is he here?' I asked, glancing towards the ward.

The nurse seemed relieved that we had a goal in mind; she stood up and led the way to the near-empty room, pulling back the curtain.

'Stay as long as you like,' she said kindly. 'No one will disturb you.'

I walked over to the body that had once been Dad, leaning over to kiss him 'goodbye' like a robot, doing what was expected. The others followed suit, and I reached out for his hand. Now I can hold his hand, I thought. My head cold no longer relevant. It wouldn't have mattered anyway, would it? I could have held his hand a few hours before – when he was alive. Now he'll never know I was here; now he'll never know I held his hand.

Dad's body felt and looked like rubber – hard, stiff and cold. He was partially curled up and facing the door; his knees were bent. The sheet was pushed down and his chest was exposed. His eyes were half open and so was his mouth. The body on the bed looked like a wax-work model of my father. There was a strange, haunted look on his face.

I thought about the medical staff who had been with Dad last. Why had they left him like this, I wondered. I wanted to see him lying flat on the bed, covered up to his shoulders with a sheet, his eyes and mouth closed in a more dignified manner. I thought back to the telephone call earlier: ' . . . come in now, Mrs Hill. Mr Hill has taken a serious turn for the worse.' I bet he'd already died when they called, I thought. All the time we were sat in the office he was dead . . . he'd died and he was here on his own and we didn't know . . .

I was cross – but with no one to blame; it was no one's fault. And now, looking down at the empty shell lying on the bed in front of us, I made a decision: 'Dad's not *in* here,' I said, indicating the body. 'He's left already. Can't you tell?' I asked the bewildered and horrified family gathered around the bed.

'I think I'm going home, as there's nothing here.' Then, pointing to my heart, I added, 'Dad's here.' It sounded cruel, but the pained expression on this curled up, motionless corpse bore no resemblance to the animated and loving energy of my dad. I was sure that Dad was no longer in this body; but where was he? I believed with all my heart that he must be somewhere . . .

As if in agreement with my assessment, music unexpectedly filled the room as both my own and Debbie's mobile phones began to ring, making us jump. The two different tunes played together, like a bad joke. We all looked at each other in amazement.

'Didn't you switch off your phone after Charlotte called?' Debbie asked.

'Yes,' I told her. 'Right after you.'

'And I saw you do it!' Dianne jumped in.

How could this be? How could both phones somehow 'coincidentally' have managed to switch themselves back on again?

Both phones had received text messages from Dad's grandchildren: 'Is Granddad OK? Tell us what's going on,' No, no I wanted to shout – Granddad is dead, he is DEAD!

'Give Granddad a kiss from me,' requested the other. But we couldn't reply.

How do you text 'Granddad died' in response? Debbie leaned over and gave Dad another kiss, this time from his grandchildren. And, as she did so, each of us was aware that if the phones hadn't turned themselves on, this final request could never have been met.

Mobiles phones don't just switch themselves on; and even if one of our phones had been *accidentally* turned back on in our handbag, how likely was it that *both* would have switched on in this way? Two different phones in two different bags – this was *no* coincidence.

I have to go home, I thought. I have to tell the children in person that Granddad died. How do you do that? What do we do now? What happens next?

Numb with grief, but conscious of the paranormal experience that had just occurred we realised collectively that Dad was giving us his first sign. He was letting us know he was alive – or perhaps that he was still aware. Dad was trying to let us know that he'd made it to the other side, just as he'd promised to do. How else could it be explained?

I was sure of one thing though, Dad was certainly no longer in that body. Dad had left the building.

The Tunnel of Light

Madeline: The journey from Cornwall that night was long and difficult. The rain fell heavily, and the roadworks were awful. There had been an accident on the motorway and the police had coned off a section of road in front of us. We sat motionless for half an hour, after which diversions took us well out of our way.

Travelling past Taunton, we noticed the needle-like obelisk on a hill away to our right. We'd passed this landmark many times in the dark, but tonight it was eerily lit up along the stonework from below. The light hit an unusually low cloud at the top of the monument transforming it into a brightly illuminated pillow all around it.

The monument now looked exactly like the tunnel that people describe when they have a 'near-death experience' – the tunnel that you pass through to reach the bright light on 'the other side' of life. The significance of the timing wasn't lost on us: maybe this was why we'd been delayed? So that we could witness the 'light at the end of the tunnel'? It was some measure of comfort to realise that if you open your eyes, and aren't closed down by your grief, there are signposts and signals all around you.

Breaking the News

Jacky: Later, we found out what happened in the moments before Dad passed. I think he'd decided enough was enough. No more of this; no more pain – and definitely no more medical procedures. The doctors had monitored Dad's heart and it was fine, but then suddenly, and without warning, he'd had a massive heart attack. Apparently, they'd tried to start his heart three times with no success.

I always imagine Dad's response on leaving his body: 'Oh, hello Eric. So it's true then – all this afterlife stuff. It's my time now is it?' Then Eric would undoubtedly have replied: 'Yes Ron, no more pain. Well done mate; what a life! Come on, let's go. You've earned your rest, and the family on the other side are waiting for you ...'

I tried to ring my husband John on the mobile, but couldn't get hold of him. Afterwards I was glad. A few more minutes and I would see him anyway. It was right to do these things face to face, if possible.

I dropped the others off first and then went home. We'd planned to gather at Mum's as soon as we were ready, to be together – to be a family . . . just one person missing.

My daughter Georgina met me on the driveway as I stepped out of the car. In some way I think she knew. I always rang and kept them up to date and this time I hadn't.

'Granddad?' she asked, searching my eyes for a clue.

'I'm so sorry. Granddad didn't make it,' I told her. 'He died,' I added, to clarify once again.

Shock registered immediately on her face and she fell into my arms, sobbing. For the first time, I cried too, knowing my husband was just through the door. I no longer had to be strong if I didn't want to be.

I walked into the living room and John looked up from the TV. I shook my head as our eyes met.

'No?' He was afraid of confusing my meaning. I lowered my eyes.

'He died,' I said, flatly, all emotion suddenly lost.

Then I walked away, abandoning him. I rushed upstairs to my eldest daughter Charlotte, who was sitting in her bedroom, awaiting my return, and told her the news.

Now both of my daughters were crying and there was nothing I could do to reassure them. No hug was *ever* going to be enough.

Georgina's boyfriend Kyle was at the house, so he took over from me, cradling Georgina in his arms and I was glad. With the stress of her granddad in hospital, Charlotte and her boyfriend Rob had bickered hours earlier and Rob had left the house. He'd been kind, and tried to comfort her, telling her, 'Your granddad will be OK; he always is', but Charlotte knew better, some instinct told her otherwise. On hearing the news, Rob immediately returned to the house and I was relieved to hand Charlotte over to him.

My husband John now didn't have a 'job' to do and looked lost – his job was to comfort me, to fix things, but I wasn't crying any more. Grief hits people in different ways, but it didn't really seem to have hit me at all.

Half an hour later, we all walked round to Mum and Dad's bungalow as we'd planned. I felt sad as I saw the SOLD sign on the board outside. Mum and Dad had reserved their beautiful retirement apartment in our village, but now Dad would never get to live in his elegant new home.

Dianne's husband Dave was in the kitchen and, as we stepped inside, he fell into my arms sobbing. My brother-in-law Dave regularly went fishing with Dad, so they were friends as well as relations. I cried because *he* cried. I was sad because I felt *his* grief, openly expressed. Then, as we parted, I recovered again quickly, quietly resigned to the situation.

'Sitting on a Rainbow'

Madeline: Driving up from Cornwall, we played a Michael Bublé CD in the car. Dad had loved this album and we'd listened to it together, just two short weeks before. The whole CD played with no problem until the song, 'I've got the World on a String'. As this track began, the music turned itself right down low and the song, much loved by Dad, played at a whisper.

It really sounded like one of us had reached up and altered

the volume, but we knew that neither of us had. Was this something else to take notice of? I listened carefully to the words Michael was singing – about having the world on a string and sitting on a rainbow; almost like looking down on the world from Heaven ... was Dad looking down on us right then? Did he have string around his finger, connecting him to us?

Was Dad telling us he'd had a good life using the words from the song? Yes, I felt it was possible that Dad was messing with the sound to let us know he was OK, that he was around. Had the song turned down low to catch our attention? It had never done this before, why would it now?

A little while later, I picked up the unmistakable smell of cigarettes in the confines of the car. Nobody we knew smoked. Yet we were both aware of this strong smell, with no obvious source. The windows were all closed, but the smell of cigarettes was undeniable. It brought back a memory from childhood – as kids we'd always complained if Dad smoked in the car, and although it had been many years since he'd done so, the smell was something we still associated with him.

What with the volume of a track carrying poignant words, the smell of cigarettes in the car and being in the right place at the right time to witness the strange column of light through the window, we had certainly experienced some weird psychic phenomena tonight on the journey. And all in the space of just a few hours – the hours since Dad's death. Three of my five senses had been alerted – sound, smell and sight. Or was it some kind of sixth sense? Interesting ...

We pulled up at Mum's house at around 1.30 a.m. Everybody was still awake and waiting for us. As we walked in the door, we fell into each other's arms. We cried and talked in quiet disbelief, all the while, taking great comfort in being together.

Everyone had a glass of 'something' in their hand and we sat and discussed future plans and our sad day. Mum told us she wanted The Carpenters' song 'On Top of the World' played at the funeral. Apparently, Mum and Dad had previously discussed this together. It was Dad's favourite.

It reminded me of the strange incident in the car earlier and the similarity in sentiment between the two songs. Having the world on a string, and sitting on a rainbow ... and Dad being 'On the Top of the World'. It was weird.

I could just imagine Dad sitting 'on top of the world' or 'on a rainbow', looking down on us right now, letting us know what a great life he'd had, and that he was still right here with us.

Alarm Clock Sign

Jacky: We sat for several more hours sharing our strange stories: the computer password; the mobile phones ringing; the light surrounding the monument and the sudden change of volume of Dad's song in the car ...

Then Dianne and Mum told us another story. The bedside alarm clock had been ringing as they entered the house at around quarter past eight.

'As Mum and I walked though the door, we could hear the alarm blaring away upstairs.' Dianne explained excitedly.

'Really? Are you sure it hadn't been set?' I asked.

'No way, why would the alarm be set for eight fifteen at night?' Dianne replied.

Then Mum added, 'No I hadn't set the alarm.'

'And it wasn't ringing when I was at the house earlier, when I came for Dad's things,' I confirmed.

'How weird. Maybe it was Dad?' Debbie suggested.

We grinned. No wonder the hospital had seemed so empty. We hadn't been at the hospital when Dad died, so he'd already come back to the house looking for us, even 'ringing us'! It made perfect sense.

Flickering Lights

I turned to Madeline as I remembered the conversation we'd had with Dad only a week and a half before; about how he'd been beckoned to leave his body by his granddad and two favourite aunties, and his out-of-body excursion.

'Do you remember me asking Dad if he would help write a book?' I asked her. Madeline nodded in agreement. 'Do you think he's started already?' I grinned. 'Perhaps we should write about his afterlife visits? I bet there will be more,' I went on, half hoping. 'We ought to write some of this stuff down.'

'Well you did ask Dad to "call" when he got to heaven,' Madeline reminded me. 'Perhaps he's begun?'

Then, right on cue, the light began to flicker above the easy chair where Madeline sat and immediately everyone laughed – a moment of lightness in the gloom and sadness. Why would the light flicker at that exact moment – as if in reply? Was it really Dad? We'd downed a few glasses of alcohol to numb the pain that night, perhaps we were making more of it than we should?

Madeline had already started writing a book about Dad's life a few years before, sharing some of his illnesses and accidents as a way of easing the pain of the experiences we'd all lived through. She'd found it too traumatic to carry on though. My 'author head' now raced ahead – I realised I would never manage a book like this alone. It was too hard. How could I relive it all again – on my own? 'Perhaps we should write a book together?' I suggested to Madeline.

'Maybe we should,' she replied, nodding in agreement.

And we were all sure that if Dad was *really* there, if he was really *alive* in some other form, he would certainly help – and if today was anything to go by, he'd already begun to do so.

PART II

The Life and Times of our Darling Dad

Chapter 4

Once upon a time...

Blessed is he who loves his brother as well
when he is afar off as when he is by his side.

St Francis of Assisi

The Early Years

Madeline: Our grandparents, James Albert Hill and Evelyn May Rowles, married in 1927. 'Our Jim' was dearly loved by his new bride's family, especially her younger sisters who found him charming and kind. Evelyn May was born in the month of May. The affectionate groom nicknamed his beautiful new wife 'Blossom', after the tree blossom which flowers during the month, a term that stuck. The rest of the family called her May.

Jim was a forester and carpenter and worked long hours on the large Eynsham Hall Estate in Oxfordshire – a fine Jacobean-style mansion. Jim regularly worked in the 30 acres of beautiful gardens and parkland. Maybe working in such spectacular surroundings gave Jim the incentive to aspire to owning his own property: the young couple made their relatives proud by buying their own bungalow, becoming the first in their family not to rent.

In 1932, Jim and May were both twenty-seven and by now had two little boys, Ron (Dad) aged two and his elder brother Eric, who was four. Money was tight, so Jim took on a second job delivering weekend newspapers door to door. With Christmas coming up, the young couple also bought a pig to fatten up and sell at the nearby farmers' market to earn some extra cash.

One day, just before Christmas, May was startled by a knock at the door. A policeman stood there, delivering horrifying news. May's young husband had fallen out of a tree on the estate and he'd broken his back. He'd been taken to the Radcliffe Hospital in Oxford, which was many miles away and extremely difficult for the young mother to visit. Tragically, Jim lived for just another three days. May was a widow at twenty-seven.

After the accident, May and her two young sons moved back in with her parents, and managed with the help of her large family – three sisters and four brothers. Two of her sisters would remain childless after their marriages and they continued to support May with the upbringing of her two young sons.

May went to work at a Blanket Mill, like her father, and grandfather before her; working as a blanket weaver at Earlys Mill, making the famous Witney blankets. She was the first woman to work two looms at the same time to earn the extra money she needed to keep her sons.

The two boys were treasured and spoiled by the extended family and helped to make up for the loss of their father. The two charming, funny and lovely boys grew into equally charming and adorable men.

At eighteen, Eric was called up to do his national service and joined the Royal Marines. When he came out, he married Joyce, a dark-haired, country girl. Later he became self-employed, upholstering furniture. Unfortunately, however, he suffered with arthritis, made worse in his hands by pulling fabric tight over the countless old armchairs he lovingly brought back to life with rich colours and new materials.

As a young man, Dad was very handsome. Early black and white photographs reveal a young, tanned Sean Connery look. He learned to drive during his national service and was given the position of private driver – batman to a lieutenant colonel in the Royal Army Ordnance Corps – a rank he took very seriously and of which he was very proud.

Dad had a part-time summer job in the early fifties, selling ice cream and regularly went to the home of his aunt and uncle to count the takings from his round. Mum was best friends with their daughter, Beryl, and would often visit too. This, of course, provided the setting for the shy couple to admire each other from afar. Dad always gave Mum an extra-large scoop of ice cream when she visited his van with her sister Marlene.

The day before her sixteenth birthday, Dad gave Mum a box of chocolates and asked her out on their first date. When she arrived home, she hid the chocolates in the piano, so her sister wouldn't find them. She knew she would've been teased mercilessly.

Dad used to cycle seven miles to pick Mum up, after which the two of them would cycle together another seven miles to the cinema. After the movie Dad would escort Mum home again, before cycling back home. It must have been love!

Mum later insisted that Dad learn to dance; she told him she would go fishing with him (his passion), if he would practise his steps – a fair exchange. He wasn't keen, but when she danced with other men who asked her, he was green with envy.

So they went to Oxford once a week and had dance lessons together. As it turned out, this powerfully built man was a fantastic dancer, and very light on his feet for someone who wore size eleven shoes.

When Dad spun Mum around the dance floor they looked graceful and elegant, and people stopped to watch. Mum was not tall – only five foot two – but with her slim, hourglass figure and fine legs, she looked stunning in her never-ending supply of ballroom dresses, while Dad, in his dinner suit, was her stylish, handsome companion: the beautiful people.

Mum and Dad married in Witney, Oxfordshire in 1954. Dad's cousin and Mum's best friend, Beryl, was bridesmaid, along with Mum's sister Marlene. Dad's beloved aunties helped out too; making the cake and wedding dress.

They were married for eight years before their first baby daughter Jacky came along – Dad's pride and joy. Then, a year later, Mum was pregnant with her second child. Proud grandmother May was to look after Jacky when Mum was in hospital giving birth. Tragically, however, May died just three weeks before Debbie was born.

Dad's precious mother had passed away at sixty years old. Dad, who was still only thirty-five, couldn't bear it, his grief so painful. Mum suggested to him that they still think of her as living in Witney, two hours away. This way Dad coped; putting his grief on hold.

Close Encounter with Death

Some years later, Dad became a sales supervisor of a large food manufacturer, responsible for six vans and drivers. One morning, a new driver started and Dad was 'showing him the ropes'. Seated on the passenger side of the van, Dad was looking down, checking paperwork. They were travelling back towards Burton on Trent, when a large Ford Zephyr smashed into them from the opposite lane. Dad was thrown through the windscreen on impact. He hadn't even braced himself; he hadn't seen it coming. This was a long time before seatbelt laws, and there were none fitted. It was a terrible crash. The local newspaper reported it under the headline: 'The Biggest Snarl-Up of Traffic Ever Recorded'.

Dad's eye socket had been broken at the bottom, and I recalled Mum telling me that his face was so swollen his eye looked like it was sitting on top of his cheek. Sixty stitches ran down one side of his face, although the other side was untouched. Mum said he looked like a cartoon monster.

By this time they had three small daughters, all under the age of six (I was still a baby). As Mum stood with the doctor in the hospital, she was scared – but she needed to know the truth.

'What's the worst that could happen?' she asked the doctor.

He considered momentarily. 'Well, there's the dislocated hip and a smashed kneecap; he's probably paralysed down one side of his face; he has a broken jaw and a broken nose, he might be blind in one eye . . . ' He paused here, before continuing: 'And he could have brain damage.'

He might just as well have slapped her, but she'd wanted to know, to prepare.

Yet, eventually, the dislocated hip was sorted, the smashed kneecap removed, and the knee sewn up without one, although he could never fully bend it again. Dad's face was indeed paralysed down one side – he used to hold his tea mug against his cheek, hoping for some sensation, not realising his skin was protesting to the heat, mottling red.

As for his eyes, although he suffered double vision for a time, his sight was satisfactorily restored. His bones mended, the skin on his face was pulled taught with the stitches, like half a facelift. Over time, he developed a natural bag under his unharmed eye, while the numb side never had one. He remained good looking, if a little craggier. Sean Connery had been replaced by Walter Matthau.

Dad recovered his wits, but lost his confidence. He was off work for six months and, during this time, he'd be picked up from home by ambulance and taken to hospital for physiotherapy.

One day the ambulance driver said to him: 'I was the driver at the scene of your crash. I remember when we got to you; we didn't know whether to drive you to the hospital or the mortuary.'

Special Dad Time

Jacky: Dad had been working long hours before the crash, so once he started to improve we had the opportunity to spend a little more time with him. On Fridays and Saturdays, when Mum worked at a local hotel (a job she loved), Dad would keep us up late, although Madeline had to go to bed just a little earlier. We relished the special time with Dad as much as Mum relished the break from her three small daughters!

Dad had begun to go fishing occasionally with the assistance of a strong friend, who would lift him down the river bank. We used to help with the less glamorous pursuit of catching worms in the garden ready for bait. We would follow Dad around the lawn, watching as he pricked holes in the muddy, damp grass with a large garden fork before pouring jugs of warm soapy water down the holes. Worms would come flooding to the surface and our job was to pick them up and collect them in a bucket. We actually delighted in the task; helping Dad made us feel grown up and important.

Unconscious but Aware

Madeline: Once Dad had fully recovered, the family moved to a small village nearer his work. He also eventually received some compensation from his accident, and we flew to Majorca – our first holiday abroad.

Going abroad back in the early 1970s was certainly unusual, and this made it a very special trip indeed. It was also an opportunity to spend some real quality time with Dad. The memories of palm trees and sunshine are still with me today, even though I was only about five years old.

After we got back, Dad continued to work ridiculously long hours, often leaving at five in the morning and arriving home after we were asleep.

One evening, while sitting in a meeting, Dad suddenly had a pain in his stomach. He lay in bed later that night with what he thought was raging indigestion. The bedroom was in darkness, when Mum stirred and reached out. Her hand came into contact with a clammy, wet sheet.

'Have you wet the bed?' she asked, totally amazed.

Dad was mortified and just as surprised as she was. 'Oh no, sorry,' he answered. 'I think I must have an upset stomach.'

'Put the light on, Ron,' Mum said, as she pulled back the covers. The patch in the bed was black, or at least very dark, spreading like a large red-wine stain. The last of Mum's sleepiness disappeared away, as it dawned on her what she was seeing.

'This is blood,' she said. 'You haven't got an upset stomach – you're passing blood.' Mum phoned the doctor who told her to give Dad a glass of milk, 'pad him up' and take him to the surgery first thing in the morning.

They did this, and Dad finally went back to sleep.

Mum, however, lay awake listening to a small noise. It was like the sound of somebody holding the neck of a balloon tightly between their fingers and releasing the air in a tiny high-pitched wail. Unbeknown to Mum, this was the sound of blood escaping through a perforated ulcer in Dad's stomach.

Suddenly, Dad jumped out of bed. 'There's something the matter,' he cried, rushing towards the bathroom.

Mum rushed after him, frantically trying to get her dressing gown on, while calling out to him: 'Don't lock the door, Ron – don't lock the door behind you.' Then she heard an almighty crash as Dad collapsed on to the bathroom floor. Mum tried the door. It was unlocked, but Dad had fallen diagonally across the length of the room, barring the entrance as effectively as the bolt would have done. She rang the doctor again.

'He's now unconscious on the bathroom floor,' she told him, terrified.

'I'll phone for an ambulance,' said the doctor. 'I'm on my way.'

The ambulance crew arrived in no time, and having managed, finally, to push the bathroom door open, they carried Dad out of the house by the light of the emerging dawn.

Spirits in the Bedroom

Jacky: I was five years old at the time of Dad's car crash, and the only one of my siblings who was old enough to recognise its full horror. Because of the way that Dad had looked, lying in that hospital bed, I'd understood all too clearly that he could have died, and this was a thought that I'd never managed to shake off. Consequently, ever since the crash, I'd suffered from nightmares and disturbed sleep, and would regularly wake up in the night to see 'people' or 'beings' in my bedroom.

The night Dad was rushed to hospital with a perforated ulcer was one such occasion, and I'd found myself in the downstairs toilet, crying and totally disorientated. I struggled back to bed and finally slept, but woke up early the next morning to a real commotion. School friends who had stayed with us overnight rushed into my bedroom to tell me that Dad was being taken into hospital *again*. I looked out of the window just in time to see him being driven away by ambulance, my trauma complete.

A 'Lucky' Accident

Madeline: With five children in the house (the three of us, plus two school friends), Mum couldn't go with Dad to the hospital. Terrified, she waited anxiously at home.

Unable to stop Dad's bleeding, the doctors finally decided, days later, to operate and remove part of his stomach. He was given a blood transfusion and, in his weakened state, he fell off the bed, bringing all the equipment down on top of him. Dad fell on his bad knee – the one he'd smashed in the car crash.

Slowly, he recovered from the stomach operation, but his diet was restricted and he continued to struggle with bouts of poor digestion. Much later, however, when he was recuperating at home, Dad discovered that his bad knee could now bend a great deal better than it ever had since the car crash. During the fall in the hospital he had somehow re-stretched the ligaments in his knee. He was now able to dance properly for the first time in many years!

Solving the Mystery

Jacky: Dad always swore that he remembered the ambulance crew arriving while he lay on the floor unconscious.

'But I *do* remember it!' he'd protest to Mum. 'As you tried to *push* the door from your side, I was trying to *pull* the door open from the bathroom side.'

'But Ron, you were unconscious!' Mum would always insist, sceptical.

Frustrated, the mystery was left unsolved until many years later I encountered the phenomenon called 'out-of-body' experience.

My first out of body experience

One night, I woke up thirsty and went downstairs for a glass of water; as I marched back up the stairs, I became detached from my physical body. With each step, I felt taller and taller, as my head floated above the rest of my body. As I walked into my bedroom, I was completely confused. I turned to look in the mirror and was amazed to discover that I was looking *down* on my reflection! I opened my wardrobe to hang up my robe, and the rail which was usually *above* my eye-level was now *below*, and I was stunned to see dust along the top of the bar. How could I see so high up, at a point which was normally above my head?

After researching information about this bizarre event, I realised I'd had an out-of-body experience, or OBE, whereby the spirit separates from the physical body. When this happens, many people report that they find themselves looking down at their bodies as they detach, and float towards the ceiling (common in heart-attack victims and those suffering bodily trauma during illnesses and accidents). After surgery, patients will tell their surgeons word for word what was said while they were under anaesthetic, or even momentarily 'dead' on the operating table.

I told Dad about my findings, offering the OBE as an explanation for what had happened that night as he lay unconscious on the bathroom floor. Dad was relieved. Everything now made perfect sense – he *had been* aware of activity around him as he lay there, and he *had* tried to open the door – just not in his physical body. Dad had experienced his first out-of-body experience the night his ulcer perforated.

OBE research

Madeline: If our conscious mind can pop in and out of the body during our lifetime, in the way that Jacky's and Dad's clearly did, surely this suggests that we are not merely bodies – that we are not limited by our physical selves, but are separate; that the soul resides in the body during this lifetime, but leaves again at death. Our soul finds the body a useful instrument here on Earth. The soul and the body are two distinct things, merged together for everyday life on Earth, but able to separate during OBEs and near-death experiences.

Mostly, OBEs happen unexpectedly, the majority occurring when people are in bed, unwell or resting or, sometimes sleeping or dreaming. An episode of fatigue, worry or shock can cause this 'awareness' (the part of you that is the 'observer') to separate briefly from the body.

Phenomena associated with OBEs can be verified by, say, viewing a previously unseen object beyond our range of vision (like the dust on a high rail in Jacky's experience, for example), an object in the next room or even somewhere outside or hearing a conversation that is taking place a considerable distance from the person concerned.

Rocket Ron

After the perforated ulcer episode, the doctors advised Dad to give up his high-pressured job or, 'We might end up burying you, after all,' they warned. The doctors also advised to him to be very careful about what he ate – this job fell to Mum!

For most of their married life, Mum was in charge. Dad was placid and compliant, and was happy for her to take the lead. After the ulcer, she watched his weight, counting every biscuit, suggesting persuasively that he should stop at two. He usually did, but like a naughty child, occasionally took an extra biscuit or an especially large slice of cake, only to suffer later with indigestion. Annoyingly for him, Mum was always right.

Dad started to work for himself. He had always been a

good salesman – charismatic and honest – and customers loved him. 'Cup of tea Ron?' They always asked when he walked in. But even so, he struggled to build up a business from scratch. Sometimes he would sell stock for a company who couldn't deliver the goods quickly enough, so that weeks would go by and unfulfilled orders would eventually be cancelled. With no commission coming in, his time and petrol were wasted, and the bills piled up.

In the meantime, there were still plenty of 'free' pursuits that we could all enjoy together, and Dad set about teaching his three little girls – Jacky aged ten, Debbie eight and me just six years old – to ballroom dance. As Joe Loss and his orchestra struck up their big-band music on the stereo in the corner of the lounge, we'd waltz around the room on the green–gold carpet, taking it in turns to hold on to Dad's large hands. While he danced with me, my sisters would try dancing with each other, squabbling over who should take the lead and be 'the man'.

As the smallest, I had to take great strides to keep up with Dad, even when he moderated his steps for me. In the end, I stepped up on to his large feet and stayed in time with him that way, travelling through the air effortlessly; determined not to look down, my chin held high, just as he'd shown us, following the footfalls from memory with immense satisfaction.

One day, a business acquaintance called to the house. He wanted Dad to sell his new range of fashion jewellery. Dad had tried to sell jewellery before, with limited success, yet this collection was different – it was younger, fresher – and Dad had a struggle on his hands to keep his three young daughters away from the trays of sparkling earrings, pretty necklaces and colourful bangles!

The range was an instant success, selling incredibly well.

Dad's sales area covered nine counties so, once again, he was away from the house for long hours. But at last, he was making some decent money.

When we were teenagers with boyfriends, Dad started to make homemade wine. The garage was home to many large, interesting bottles and pipes, gurgling and bubbling away. Occasionally, just as we'd settled down to watch the telly for the evening, loud bangs could be heard from the direction of the garage. Corks would then shoot from their bottles and wine would explode all over the ceiling. Dad's wine became known as 'Rocket Fuel' and, in a natural progression from this, Dad acquired a new nickname: 'Rocket Ron'.

Dad frequently received boxes of jewellery samples through the post. Nick and Dad used to take the large elastic bands from around the packages and stretch them over their faces, distorting the skin into funny shapes. They would look at each other and then in the mirror at the ugliness they'd created; a squashed nose, a bent ear, and hoot with laughter like a couple of school boys.

Dad would get his eyebrows caught in the bands and they would both roar louder still. He used to hold his face, the numb side, with one hand, his other hand on his thigh for support as he folded double in hysterics. Mum and I would roll our eyes and mutter to each other, but finally their delight would become infectious and we'd fall about laughing with them, despite the silliness.

Uncle Eric

Jacky: Eric was one of our favourite uncles. He was hilarious. He bore an uncanny resemblance to the UK TV comic, Eric

Morecambe. I remember him pinching his glasses on one side and jiggling them up and down – the impersonation of the comedian complete.

We didn't see Uncle Eric and Aunty Joyce very often while we were growing up because of the two-and-a-half-hour drive that separated us. Dad always smoked in the car and this made us all sick on the journey. We always started out in pretty dresses, ready to visit our many aunts and uncles in the Witney area, yet arrived, more often than not, dressed only in a cardigan and towel, clothes shed along the way as they became splashed with the regurgitated contents of our breakfast. The journey with their small, car-sick daughters became too challenging for Mum and Dad to make on a regular basis.

Madeline: My wedding was the only one that Uncle Eric and Aunty Joyce managed to attend. As I walked into the church in my wedding dress, Uncle Eric was sitting directly ahead. I focused on Eric's face as he smiled up at me, and I saw the tears of pride running down his cheeks. I adored these lovely men – Dad and his brother Eric.

Jacky: There was a period of time when it seemed as though *every* time Joyce or Eric rang it was to bring the sad news that one of Dad's and Eric's many aunts and uncles had died. So when Joyce called one day with yet more bad news, we were totally unprepared for it to be about Uncle Eric who had died in his sleep. He was just sixty-three years old. We were devastated.

Eric died before I felt I'd really had time to get to know him. But death for Eric wasn't the end of his life. Soon he was visiting us again – from the 'other side'.

Madeline: I named my first son after our much-loved Uncle Eric. Samuel Jack Eric never knew his great uncle – not on *this side* of life, anyway. However, at sixteen weeks old, Sam started to chuckle and burble at something unseen in the corner of my darkened bedroom during a night feed. He stared, transfixed at one spot just past the bottom of the bed, as if fascinated, a huge grin on his little face. He nodded at the darkness and acknowledged 'the visitor' with a stream of unintelligible chat and laughter. Who was responsible for these and other night-time giggles? Uncle Eric always got the 'blame'. Children, it seems, are often more open than adults to this kind of spiritual experience.

Many years later, we were *still* 'inviting' Eric to all of our family events, sharing a joke with him and including him in our conversations; he often seemed to respond with a flickering light.

Jacky: Eric's death somehow made Dad seem more fragile to us. Dad, however, had a number of years of good health ahead of him. That is, until a year and a half before he was seventy, when everything changed dramatically.

Chapter 5

Heaven can wait

It's not that I'm afraid to die; I just don't want to be there when it happens.

Woody Allen

Here We Go Again

Madeline: 'Now, I don't want you to worry ...' My mother's words down the phone line were an obvious reason *to* worry, I thought, uneasily. 'We've just got back from the hospital.'

I knew about Dad's appointment with the optician and how they had referred him to the hospital. 'And?' I asked, my voice steady, guarded.

'There is a growth near the bottom of his brain,' she explained, then added hastily, 'but it's *not* a tumour.'

I sat down on the chair in the corner of the bedroom and steeled myself. The room was shadowy, but a few shafts of sunlight slipped through the gap in the long curtains, picking up tiny specks of dust, which spiralled around on an unde-tectable air current.

My God, *of course* it was a tumour. Something was grow-ing in Dad's brain that shouldn't be there. I felt numb. 'What can I do?' I asked.

'Absolutely nothing.'

'Shall we come up?'

'There's no point; not until we know when he's going in. Come up *then*,' said Mum.

I hung up the phone, but stayed perfectly still. Dad was only sixty-eight years old. He'd outlived his brother Eric by several years, he was older than his mother had been and had sur-passed the age his father had reached by decades. But still, we certainly weren't ready to let him go yet. I felt apprehension creeping into my stomach and up to my chest. I was grateful the room was still dim; sunshine didn't seem appropriate.

Despite what Mum had said, we decided to travel up to the Midlands in any case. I wanted to see Dad – to reassure myself that he was up for this, that he was strong enough for the necessary operation.

Illumination

Often we'd get together at Mum and Dad's as a family to play a card game of gin rummy or Newmarket. We'd use a score pad to draw sketches of the fantasy prizes for first, second and third place – usually something like this: first prize – win-ning lottery ticket or a luxury villa with pool; second prize – a new car or some fishing tackle (if pencilled in for Dad); third prize, which always fell short of expectations – a hastily drawn ice lolly or a pair of pants!

'Uncle Eric would have found this hysterical, wouldn't he?' Jacky once reflected, silly humour being his speciality. And right on cue, as if Eric had replied, the wall light flickered in the room, and everyone laughed.

'Good timing, Uncle Eric!' said Debbie, and the light flickered once more.

A few weeks earlier, five of us sat at the breakfast-room table; Debbie called over for a couple of hours, and we dished out the playing cards. Dad wasn't playing well, and we all groaned as he added a third king to the pile on the table for the next person to pick up.

Mum was getting impatient with Dad. 'Oh Ron,' she moaned. 'Could you please check what's on the table before you throw away?'

'Well,' he protested, 'I can't see what's there.'

'Move chairs then, will you? Look, sit under the light,' she instructed.

But it made no difference and Dad peered down at the table, squinting.

'I don't understand why you can't see the cards; you've only just got new glasses,' complained Mum, deciding there and then to send him back to the optician. He *did* go back to the opticians a week or two later, and they referred him to the local hospital. The hospital looked *through* his eyes and recognised the problem. Brain scans soon proved them unbearably right.

Our visit was all too brief and, as we packed up the car for our return journey, to Cornwall, Dad stood in the doorway.

'This might be the last time I see you,' he said quietly,

I felt angry with him, cross that he would 'voice' what I wanted to keep hidden.

'Don't say that; don't *ever* say that.'

'Well, you never know what's going to happen.' His voice had a gentle, Cotswold resonance, a quality I'd always loved. He looked lost. I hugged him.

'We'll be back up to see you as soon as you go in. You'll be fine,' I sounded strong, but I didn't feel it.

Mum was composed, or at least she gave a good performance. It wasn't the first time she'd had to be brave. It all sounded so awful, so shocking. Yet I had no idea of the ordeal that was to come.

The date for Dad's surgery was set: Friday, 1 April – April Fools' Day.

'Shall we come up?' I asked again.

'Wait till he goes in. It might be cancelled yet; you know what hospitals are like,' said my ever-practical mother. But the operation wasn't cancelled and Dad went in as planned.

The day passed in a blur. To take my mind off Dad's operation, we visited a smart café, but all I noticed was the big-band music playing in the background. I was six years old again, dancing on Dad's feet . . .

Relief

The telephone rang on Saturday morning following the operation. I ran to pick it up. 'Hello?' I was breathless.

'Hello, my darling.'

'Oh my God. DAD!' Confusion scrambled my thoughts. 'What's happening?'

'The surgeon says I'm doing fine. I've come for a little walk along the corridor and I thought I'd ring you.'

The surgeon had operated just the day before. Mum had

already confirmed it'd gone well, but I didn't expect *this*.

'I can't believe you're up,' I said, relief flooding through me. 'How do you feel?'

'I feel fine.'

'Oh, thank God.' I almost sobbed the words, but held it together, just. My son Samuel had come into the room and looked at me questioningly. I gave him a big grin and a thumbs-up sign.

He was fine, he was fine; HE WAS FINE! I wanted to be there – now. Everybody else was there. I wanted to hug him, to celebrate. I wanted to share the news. I quickly dialled everyone I could think of, *anybody* who had worried with me or cared about him.

I slept well on Saturday night; speaking to Dad on the telephone was such a relief and, evidently, good for winding down after so much worry. I rang Mum first thing Sunday morning. It was still quite early.

'And how is he this morning?' I enquired, cheerfully.

'I haven't rung the hospital yet. They'll still be doing breakfasts, I should think. We're going over in a couple of hours; Jacky's picking me up. I've bought him a fishing magazine.' I smiled at this. 'I've still got *so* much to do,' she added. 'Do *you* want to ring the hospital?' I scribbled down the number, then hung up before dialling the ward.

Not So Good Today

'Hello, I wonder if you can tell me how Ron Hill is today?'

A weary female voice responded, 'Just a moment please.' I pressed the receiver closer to my ear, but could hear no chatter, no discussion – perhaps she'd flicked me to mute.

The same voice came back on the line, but this time more cautious.

'Who's calling please?'

'It's his daughter.'

'One moment please,' she said again.

I started to feel a little uneasy now, and pressed the phone harder to my ear, but could only hear my own heart, beating back at me.

'I'm afraid Mr Hill's not so good this morning,' said a new voice, well informed, but tense. 'We couldn't wake him. He's being taken back down to theatre.' What was happening? What did she mean? 'I'm afraid he's unconscious . . . ' My heart was now so loud it was competing with her words and I strained to understand. 'We need to operate again.'

The room around me shifted slightly, as I realised I had to relay these facts to my unsuspecting family.

'Right, thank you.' I crashed down the phone noisily, then waited only a moment as endless questions rushed through my mind. Did I really have to report this? Shouldn't somebody have telephoned us? I didn't know. All I knew was that I had that feeling back in the pit of my stomach – the fear that I was ready for *yesterday*, that I had prepared for *yesterday*, hadn't arrived. Now unexpectedly, it lashed out, kicking away solid ground, but I didn't have time for it to engulf me. I was to be the bearer of bad news. I wanted to give over this responsibility to another, to make someone else ring the hospital, to find out the facts that I had woefully neglected to collect. I dialled my mother's number.

Once again, we prepared to travel to the Midlands. I explained to Sam that I needed him to be *really* good on the journey. He always was, but I was frightened; I felt so thinly drawn, stretched and taut.

Finally, we were ready to go. I threw some small toys into a box and placed it on the back seat, hoping it would keep Samuel occupied. I still felt tightly strung, like a pearl necklace that might break apart with a tilt of the head. Rain started to fall steadily, the wipers beating relentlessly. Sam played quietly and baby Jim slept on.

It was dark when we arrived; the clock on the dash glowed green: 10:15pm. The headlights picked out the diagonal rain as we pulled on to the driveway. Dad's car was there. I hadn't considered that one of my sisters would have driven him to the hospital. When his old, cherished Granada was on the drive, to me, it meant Dad was home.

They'd operated *again* on Sunday morning, after I'd telephoned. Dad was now unconscious in critical care; lost in a deep coma.

Hello, My Darling

We travelled to the hospital through the early-morning traffic. The rain from the night before had cleared, but an ominous dark cloud threatened that more was to come. April showers.

Debbie and I rang the buzzer to the ward and waited. A fresh-faced, ponytailed nurse, in a crisp blue uniform came to the door.

'We're here to see Ron Hill,' I told her. I felt apprehensive, unsure what to expect.

The room was hushed and shuttered, the patients were silent – either asleep or in a coma, I didn't know which. The only noise was the occasional bleep. Curtains were drawn around some of the patients for privacy, the open ones revealed complex machinery and monitors at both sides of the bed. Dad was in the bed straight ahead of us. His eyes were closed, his body still. He was wired up to various pieces of equipment. Frighteningly, a tube vanished deep into his skull. He looked pale, but his frame looked large and strong. We came in close.

'Dad, it's me ... it's Madeline.'

His eyes fluttered and opened briefly.

'Hello, my darling.' The quietest whisper; the first words he'd said since Saturday. I burst into tears of joy. He's OK, I thought. A nurse rushed over, concerned and Debbie explained:

'He spoke! Madeline's here and he spoke to her!' She was beaming.

To us it was momentous. The nurse seemed unimpressed. She asked us to speak quietly and we nodded guiltily, grinning. For the rest of the visit Dad didn't open his eyes again or speak any more, but there had been progress. We phoned home and reported the news.

Faith Healing

Sitting next to Dad's bed, we filled in time by sending him hands-on healing, or rather, in this case, hands-off. Whatever label you want to give it – faith healing, spiritual healing – I was drawing on 'energy' from somewhere else and directing it towards the motionless figure on the bed.

My sisters and I had learned the ancient healing art of Reiki and I'd done my first Reiki 'attunement', on a bright summer's morning, sitting at the base of the sacred and spiritual five-thousand-year-old Silbury Hill in Wiltshire. Since then, I'd been captivated by all manner of alternative healing techniques. 'Intent' was the important factor, so I imagined bright, gentle showers of healing light sprinkling down on Dad.

Whatever we were sending through our hands had an interesting effect. Dad's monitors started to bleep and a nurse came running over, looking concerned. Having checked everything thoroughly, nothing seemed out of place, so she simply reset his monitors and walked away. Our energy was *real* enough to have had a measurable influence and this was to be the first of many similar events while Dad was in a coma. We were extremely excited and used the technique at every visit.

Healing Groups Around the World

Jacky: I joined internet groups around the world, people who understood my growing interest in 'the paranormal' and alternative healing. An intimacy grew with these new 'friends' who I'd never actually met and, before long, I was sharing with them my concerns about Dad.

Prayer and healing groups were growing; linking hands around the world. I enquired as to whether anyone was able to 'send' distant healing of any sort and a lot of people offered. Many added Dad's names to their healing lists and prayed for him in churches and religious centres of all kinds. I'd read somewhere that prayer made a measurable difference to the sick, and then later read another report saying it made no difference, but we pressed on regardless. In addition, I practised my own healing, running my hands a few inches above his unconscious body, pleased to have something to do during the long visiting hours.

'Why don't we bring in photographs of him, and stick them on the wall above his bed?' I suggested to Madeline. 'What about one of him dancing? Or in his Masonic suit?' I got excited by this idea. 'We need to show Dad as *vibrant* and full of life,' I explained. And both Madeline and I felt this would help the staff think of him differently.

A Small Moment of Eternal Bliss

Early one evening, I walked in my garden, under a trellised walkway which was smothered with climbing plants. Barefoot, I stepped over fallen rose petals on warm grass. Someone, somewhere had 'injected' me with a light, I felt healed and restored. My 'vacuum' of the last few weeks had been prised opened and with enormous relief I stepped out into Eden; this moment of 'connection' helped to make the next few weeks bearable.

Confusion

Madeline: Early the following week, Dad was moved from the critical-care ward and placed on a lower-staffed side ward. Slowly, Dad had started to regain consciousness. But then, as the week went on, Dad became drowsier and less coherent. On the Friday, Mum tried to engage him in conversation.

'What have you been doing today?' Mum enquired.

'I've had breakfast with my bride!' Dad was clearly not referring to *her*.

Puzzled, Mum asked who he thought *she* was. 'You're Joseph,' was the bizarre reply.

A little later, when Debbie arrived, she asked him: 'Dad, who am I?'

'You're a pain in the arse!' was his eloquent response! It was completely out of character for this mild-mannered gentleman. It was clear there was a problem.

Finally, the hospital staff acknowledged things were *still* not right, and the operating theatre beckoned once more ...

A Psychic Connection

Jacky: Each night, while at home in bed, I wished, imagined and *believed* that I was holding Dad's hand in hospital, my soul aching to be by his side. In one powerful 'dream', I sat by Dad's bed as he slept. It was so hauntingly real, that in the morning I could still feel Dad's hand in mine, the heat, the weight, every crease and line of his large palm pressed against my own.

I wondered if Dad's being in a coma might have set his spirit free to interact with mine, like an unconscious out-of-body-experience. Research for my books had shown that people felt their loved ones touch their shoulder or hold their hand, *after* they'd 'passed over'. My soul *had* truly been with him. I *really* believed it, so maybe this was something similar?

In the meantime, I was sure that Mum was playing a crucial role. 'Without you,' I told her, 'Dad would be dead.' And the others all agreed. The tube that the surgeon had inserted into Dad's skull to drain off fluids from the operation site would regularly block. Sometimes the hospital staff sat Dad in a chair by the bed; they felt that he was asleep most of the day, but it was impossible to wake him. The busy staff changed shifts several times a day, and no one realised that Dad lay in a coma most of the time. Yet Mum was aware of every minute change in the health of the man she'd known intimately for almost all of her life.

Help From 'The Other Side'

Night after night, in my bed at home, I was able to 'see' Dad asleep in the hospital bed. Dad was never alone, and in my visions I could see a crowd of deceased family members along with other spirit-type figures surrounding his hospital bed. It was like they were holding healing sessions of their own. I always recognised at least *some* of the healers; Eric, of course, Dad's Uncle Erne, his mum and various aunts. I was surprised to see my father-in-law Jack too, but one night Eric explained his presence to me in my dream: 'We are honoured to have a master healer in our midst. He's helping us with your dad.'

Wow, a master healer? We think, like Shakespeare, that our loved ones become 'food for worms' when they die, yet here were my own relatives not only 'alive' in their own way, but with responsibilities, jobs and capabilities far beyond anything we could understand on *this* side of life. My father-in-law, a marketing director in life, was a high-ranking spirit in death – a healer, no less. Thank you, I thought. Thank you for your help.

I never doubted the validity of these night-time experiences.

A Rollercoaster Ride

Madeline: More operations followed. Then Dad was back in critical care. Mum rang to let us know the bad news: he had meningitis. Over the weekend his right lung collapsed.

I raged and cried; I was frightened all the time. We all wanted to get off this 'ride' – this never-ending up-and-down journey.

As sisters, we became closer, unified in our shrunken, insular world, not daring to look to the future, living hour by hour, minute by minute. And our foreboding proved acutely well-founded when, four weeks and two days after he entered the hospital, Dad's other lung collapsed and he was placed on a life-support machine.

Music for the Soul

Jacky: We spent weeks chatting to Dad as if he were awake and aware; telling him everything that was happening in our day-to-day lives. I always believed that somewhere in the depths of his unconscious mind there was a small part that was listening, and that if ever hypnotised, those conversations would still be there.

Talking to Madeline one evening I remarked, 'I know if we keep chatting to Dad, we'll get through to him eventually.'

'I heard one interesting case, where the unconscious person believed they were joining *in* the conversation they could hear,' Madeline recalled. 'It wasn't until the relative speaking to them told them, "You need to wake up from your coma now", that they realised they *weren't* taking part in the dialogue at all.' Madeline recalled when Dad appeared to have experienced leaving his body when he was lying unconscious on the bathroom floor after his ulcer perforated. I'd had my first OBE whilst feeling poorly, but fully awake. How do we explain the fact that I could see the dust on the top of the wardrobe rail, which was above my physical eye line?

'I've heard about people who've been roused from unconsciousness by the voice of a loved one, or a favourite celebrity . . . or even music.' I continued, 'Shall we try it?'

Slowly, Dad started to breathe by himself again, and was taken off the life-support machine, yet he remained in a coma. None the less, we recorded all of Dad's favourite music tracks, and 'plugged him in' to headphones for when we ran out of conversation. Dad reacted instantly, playing an invisible piano on the bed sheets with his fingers and conducting with his hands to The Carpenters. The music did reach him, although his eyes remained closed.

Kick A Man When He's Down

Madeline: Dad was now conscious, but he continued to slip in and out of a coma.

More operations followed: a tracheotomy, then a permanent tube was put into his head – his sixth brain operation. Then he caught the super-bug MRSA, before finally falling out of bed and breaking his pelvis.

I waited for news in my strangely suspended world. I was afraid to think at all; I was suspicious of hope, yet shunned despair. Back in Cornwall, I cried for days, convinced we would never play cards again . . . never dance.

The Healing Arts

Jacky: I continued to 'dream' about the spirit visitors at the hospital. Sometimes we spoke, and at other times I was a mere observer as they worked on Dad, healing him in teams.

Dad's Uncle Erne had been an important figure in life – an upstanding citizen in the Witney area where they lived. He was clerk to the Witney Town Council and had lived in a big town house.

Erne and his wife had a daughter with multiple sclerosis; she had been confined to a wheelchair for years. And as much as Uncle Erne presented an exterior of total propriety and conventionality, when it came to his daughter he would do anything to ease her life.

Erne had called on spiritual healers from Devon in the south of England to visit his daughter and work on her frail body. He also enlisted the help of a Chinese acupuncturist and called on other 'alternative' healers too. Uncle Eric, Dad's brother used to help and even used the acupuncturist himself. Eric 'believed' too, and wore a copper bangle on the advice of Uncle Erne which he swore helped his arthritis.

Our uncle and great uncle were way ahead of their time, defying the commonly held perception at the time that alternative healing was the domain of new-age 'hippies'. When working with these healing arts, Great Uncle Erne called on the assistance of a Native American spirit guide – from the 'other side'.

Meanwhile, I could feel them, night after night. I sensed them and saw them. We were not alone.

A ghost in the machine

Madeline: It was interesting to find out later that Uncle Erne had started the family tradition of healing, long before we, his great nieces, began practising it.

We continued to send Dad healing; he needed all the help he could get. Often, it would send the machines haywire, bringing nurses running from all directions. This invisible energy seemed to have a profound effect on something, at least.

A Revelation

Jacky: My dreams and visions told me that Dad was going to be fine, that he *would* make it through what we hoped would be his last operation. As we all sat talking or browsing through magazines in the awful visitors' waiting room at the hospital, I hatched a plan: to practise healing while meditating.

For two hours, I sat with my eyes closed. Throughout, I felt a connection with Uncle Eric and Uncle Erne. Only this time, there was a third energy I didn't recognise, although I heard the name 'Uncle John Rowles' – a cousin of Dad's. Was he dead too? I wondered. I didn't know, but later discovered he was. It was great confirmation for me, though sad for his family, it validated my experiences. Here was some information that I didn't know about in advance, therefore it was proof that what I was experiencing was real. Then suddenly, I came to and jumped up.

'Dad's out of the operation now,' I announced. 'And he's going to be OK.'

Everyone trailed after me down the corridor in response to my bizarre statement. No one questioned how I knew. And as we got to the end of the hallway, we saw Dad being wheeled out of the operating theatre. Hallelujah!

An hour or so later he awoke. He was still drowsy and slow, but this time it didn't seem to matter. He was on the path back to us – that long and winding road. This operation marked the turning point for him and he finally began to recover.

For his last night in hospital, Dad was placed on the geriatric ward. He was now quite aware and didn't want people to think he was elderly and confused like the others on the ward. He was also concerned about being allowed to leave, and said to us, 'But what if they don't let me come home?'

'Don't worry Dad,' we told him, laughing. 'If they don't sign you out, we'll kidnap you!'

On the following morning, we arrived to pick him up. As we whizzed him down the corridor in the hospital wheelchair, Dad was joyfully shouting, 'Escape from Alcatraz!'

Finally, we had him back. He was frail, pale and had lost a third of his body weight, he could only walk short distances with a walking frame or had to be pushed in a wheelchair, but he was *ours* and we were taking him home at last. It was time to start living again.

Chapter 6

It's a wonderful life

Here is the test to find whether your
mission on Earth is finished. If you're alive,
it isn't.

Richard Bach

A Full Recovery

Madeline: 'Five, four, three, two, one ...' Party poppers exploded everywhere sending coloured string around the room.

'Happy new year!' we all chorused. 'Happy new year, everybody! Happy new year, Dad.' I raised my glass to Dad in a formal salute.

Dad was sitting in his favourite Parker Knoll recliner chair and raised his glass, a smile on his face and a twinkle in his eye, as he cheered with the rest of us. He'd been home six months.

I'd never been so happy to ring in the new year – 1999 had

been the worst year of my life. Now, I was standing with a glass in my hand, and a party dress on. It felt really symbolic to throw out the old year and we all enthusiastically welcomed the dawn of the new Millennium.

Dad was sharper, quicker now. As his brain recovered and repaired, the bolt slowly slid back from his locked-off mind, so that he now began to keep up and join in – he usually even picked up the jokes *first* time round now. He was stronger too, walking unaided and, unbelievably, he was back to driving his car!

I had travelled up to see Dad again soon after he'd been 'kidnapped' from hospital. One evening, we asked him if he would like to join our card game, and much to our surprise and delight he said he would.

Midway through our third hand, we were interrupted by the telephone. Mum answered and spoke briefly to Debbie before handing the receiver to me.

'Hello?'

'Hi, I hear you're having a game of cards. Dad's not playing is he?'

'Yes. He is.'

'Madeline, how's he getting on? Is he managing? Does he remember what to do?'

'Debbie, he's thrashing us!' I told her, grinning into the telephone.

'He isn't? Really?' I could hear her scepticism.

'Yes, really! He really is!'

Debbie was choked up. 'I can't believe it,' she sniffed.

'I know,' I smiled. 'We never thought we'd see *this* again.'

'I'm coming over!' she said, suddenly. 'I'll see you in ten minutes.' This was something she had to see for herself.

The Spiritual Lesson

Jacky: I realised that we girls had 'grown' a lot spiritually since Dad's illness had begun. We were closer now than ever, and for us too, other skills had begun to appear.

One day, after Dad had been home for a little while, I said to him, 'Thanks for teaching us about unconditional love, Dad.'

He replied, 'That's all right, my darling.'

I have no idea if he really understood what I meant at the time, but he never questioned it for one moment. It was as if I was talking to his *soul* and his *soul* was the one that answered me.

Meanwhile, the spirit visitors who'd begun to appear when Dad was in hospital were still around. Each of us sisters had seen relatives in dreams, but the memories of specific instances faded in time.

Debbie and I went to see a local medium around this time; she was a psychic who specialised in talking to the deceased. I'd been for psychic readings at spiritual fayres, but never at someone's house. Chatting in the car on the way there, we'd decided that we would love it if Eric were to 'come through' for the medium, and maybe Mum and Dad's friend, Pat, who'd died just six months before. Pat had visited Dad in hospital; it seemed strange now that Dad had survived and Pat had passed on. And, we wondered, maybe our grandmother, Mum's mother would be able to visit too?

As it happened, the medium gave us the name Pat shortly after we sat down in her reading room. She described her personality so well. At the same time, she told me that I would be a successful writer. Strangely, I had just begun to work on my first book, so this was encouraging news indeed! Then we moved to a small card table which had felt-tipped letters stuck down in a circle: it was an Ouija board, a method of communication with the other side.

Ouija boards were originally created as a game, a fun way to 'communicate with the afterlife'. A working board (usually around the size of a piece of typing paper) displaying the letters of the alphabet, the numbers zero to nine and the words 'yes' and 'no' was used as the base, and a glass, or wooden, pointer was placed into the centre of the board. A group of people each place one finger onto the pointer and their energy, with the help of the spirits, was used to move the pointer around the board. As the pointer moved to different letters it spelt out words – words communicated by the spirit world. The medium we visited had created her own version and we were about to try it for ourselves.

We all placed our fingers on the pointer and it immediately spelled out ERIC. Questions revealed a series of answers, many of which we hadn't even considered. Often, the medium took her hand off the pointer. Were we mediums too? We had no difficulty in spelling out words with the help of the spirits.

It's one thing having spirit visitors appear in dreams and 'visions', but this was something else. The best proof yet. Spirits were real, and they were helping us constantly. Death was not the end, and they were proving it over and over again.

More Evidence

Madeline: I had also been to visit a medium in Cornwall, but this was many years earlier – even before Eric had died. I'd gone out of curiosity and, because the medium in question had trained at the London Psychic College, I felt confident. She'd impressed me with her information, not least by giving me only one name – Mum's.

Later, after Eric passed I visited local Mind, Body and Spirit fayres, and was nearly always picked out by mediums or psychics at the demonstrations. They always told me the same thing: 'You have a large soul group.' Well, that's nice, I always thought.

Once, a medium from Somerset, told me, 'I've got a relative here; he's on your father's side of the family.'

'Right, OK.'

'He looks smart, in a black suit, and he's carrying a small briefcase.'

'I have an idea who that might be,' I said loudly, so the rest of the audience could hear me clearly. Black suit and small briefcase; immediately I thought about the Freemasons.

'And he practises funny handshakes,' he went on, demonstrating a 'funny handshake' by comically holding his hand under his knee. Then he asked me, 'Do you get my meaning? Are you catching my drift?'

I knew immediately, and acknowledged that I would accept this relative. This was definitely a Masonic handshake joke, and the gentleman on my father's side was Dad's and Eric's dear Uncle Erne.

The medium continued to give me small pieces of information, things that would be inconsequential to anyone else: 'You have a leaking tap on your bath; the window in the kitchen is sticking, isn't it? You've got up in the night lately, haven't you, and gone downstairs when you couldn't sleep? You *are* aware of spirit aren't you? It's OK; you can just talk to them . . .' I was amazed as the tiny details kept coming, answering 'Yes' to each and every statement. Of course, many people have a leaking tap or a sticking window, but not one detail given to me that night was incorrect.

My knowledge about the afterlife continued to grow, and I bought books about it and studied it from different perspectives. I also carried on going to psychic workshops and spoke about the subject at length – with anyone who would listen.

Celebrating Life

Jacky: As the year 2000 drew on into spring and then summer, Dad became stronger and stronger and, as his seventieth birthday approached in September, we decided we needed to mark the occasion in style – by treating him to a flying lesson!

The little red and white plane beckoned. Dad was very excited. After a few minutes, he was permitted to take the controls, 'flying high', both literally and metaphorically with delight at his recovery.

Photographs recorded this remarkable feat – all the more amazing considering the nursing staff had thought he would live the rest of his life as an empty shell. As I watched him soar, I remembered the health worker at the village cottage hospital who'd suggested that Mum might need to put Dad in a care home. But just look at him now, I thought. Who would have thought that Dad would live to do such a thing?

Connecting with the Past

Madeline: I waited expectantly at the window of the elegant residents' lounge until I saw Dad's old Granada pull round the back of the hotel and into the car park. Dad was in full suit and tie, Mum was in a pretty summer blouse and skirt, with a smart navy blazer. They looked splendid.

We were staying in Morton-in-Marsh, and Mum and Dad knew every town and village in the area. This was Dad's childhood haunt, and everywhere we visited he told us stories about when he was a boy.

We found a secret ruined manor house from medieval times, hidden behind a church: Minster Lovell. The River Windrush cut past the edge of the site and it was quite fast flowing after the rain. Dad told us he had fished the Windrush as a young man, and had even swum in it; what I hadn't realised was that Mum's older brother Billy had drowned in it, aged just ten. I knew the story, of course, but hadn't known it was *here* at Minster.

Mum was only six when he'd died and didn't have many recollections of him. She did remember one Christmas though, when they'd woken early. Billy had found some of his presents, but Mum couldn't find any of hers. It was too early to wake their parents, so Billy told her kindly, 'You can choose one of mine.' Years later, our grandmother had had the recurring nightmare that her son Billy would drown, and it had happened exactly as she'd predicted.

We visited Aunty Joyce and she told us where Dad's father, Jim, was buried – surprisingly, something Dad had never known. He had never visited the grave, as he was only two when his father died. We found the church and eventually discovered a tiny stone marking the site; we gathered at the graveside and held a moment's silence to honour the grandfather I'd never known. We left feeling pleased with ourselves, touched, in no small way, to have connected Dad, aged seventy, with his *own* father.

Jacky 'The Angel Lady'

Jacky: Throughout this time, I had been reading more and more books about psychic phenomena. I was fascinated by the paranormal, but was keen to present a more positive side to the public. I'd read too much about the scarier side of the unknown. Our family experiences with the 'other side' had all been positive and life-changing – life-*saving* even.

So I set to work on my plan: to share my own and other people's wonderful real-life stories – comforting experiences of communication from the other side of life. I planned a whole series of books, and had also by now started my own magazine column. I was named 'The Angel Lady', and people were writing to me from all over the world asking for answers to their paranormal queries. Although I wasn't using my new-found psychic abilities, I was certainly able to help. My extensive research into psychic phenomena, including visits from guardian angels and spirits, as well as my own background gave me lots of help.

Dad was fascinated and often asked questions, but although he liked us talking about his brother Eric, I'm not sure he truly believed it all a hundred per cent at this stage. He *wanted* to believe it was true, but then there was the slight 'embarrassment' factor. What would other people think?

I received many letters from readers about past lives and began to research this too. I was asked questions like, 'If I'm going to another place after I die, does it mean I came from somewhere before?' Or: 'I've visited a part of the world I'd never been to before, yet I was able to direct our whole party, and tell them where the ancient sites had been – even down the back alleys, off the tourist track. Have I been there in a past life?'

I also loved reading about young children in remote Indian villages who recalled people and places they had never been to or known – and the findings of Western scientists who followed up their stories, tracking each one. In numerous cases, children were taken the many miles to visits these 'past-life' families, and were able to name family members they'd recognised from 'previous lives'.

Could I have lived before too? I wondered.

As part of my research for an article I asked a past-life regressionist to put me in a hypnotic trance. I'd never been hypnotised before, and although I was in a very relaxed state, I was still unsure as to whether it would work. The whole while I thought this, however, I was able to answer the questions none the less. It was as if my mind was now working on two different levels:

'Where are you?'

How should I know? 'Oh, I'm standing by a beautiful door.'

'Do you want to go in? Can you?'

I'm scared. The master will whip me. 'I'm not allowed.'

'It's OK; no one will see you. What's your name?'

Pollyanna, Pollyanna but they call me Moll. 'Molly, Moll.'

'What do you see?'

'It's beautiful; pretty things.' This was the lady's room, but not any more. She's in bed, taken ill. No one see's her but her maid . . .

'Have you been in this room before?'

'No.' The black maids don't go in the family rooms. I'm scared I want to leave.

As I came out of the regression, the hypnotist asked me, 'What did you learn from that life?'

I replied immediately, confident: 'No more lives as servants!'

Over the few days after this session, I 'remembered' more and more of this bizarre past life. I was in Alabama. I have no idea of the date. The Master would rape the servants, kick the dogs and horses. I got pregnant and my baby was sent to live with my mother, many miles away. I never saw my son again. I had a hard life, I recalled.

My sister Dianne and I read extensively about the phenomenon and how to regress *ourselves*, using past-life regression pre-recorded cassette tapes. Later, we regressed each other, using our own script, learning as we went along. I found myself drowning as a sailor once, and another time I was a rich, fat merchant in the Far East. My family gathered around my bed as I died, but I didn't feel any sadness. I'd earned a healthy living and I knew they would miss it when I'd gone! I really felt I had lived these lives – or at least that my soul had.

Past-life Regression Research

Madeline: I had done my own research many years earlier, back in 1992. I'd sent away for some regression tapes – a do-it-yourself past-life discovery set. At first, I was nervous, but the experiences I had at home were fascinating and stayed with me for a long time afterwards. I too bought many books on the subject and, eventually, reincarnation became the most sensible and obvious answer to how the world worked!

Researching the family tree stood me in good stead a

little later when I wanted to do research of a similar kind. When my sisters began 'regressing' family and friends, I sat in on many sessions, recording information. A date or detail of costume would help me with my research later. I would silently write down a question for the hypnotist during the session to ask for the information that I needed for my research.

I took the facts from these sessions and went away to see if the information matched the general history of any time or place. I found it easy to check census information, something now familiar to me, and clarified and agreed all kinds of interesting facts. I spent hours on the internet; always coming up with small pieces of evidence, things that accurately tied information together.

History was a strong point for me and I was passionate about discovering the 'proof' behind these sessions. I felt compelled to find any truths which might make these regressions more scientific. Dates were often difficult to pinpoint, but style of dress and types of occupation were easier to research. I had a case study of a gentleman with a moustache, in a suit, hat, and black and white shoes with a button detail at the side; he carried a silver-topped cane and worked as a clerk. He had a wife he called Kitty, two daughters, Lilly and Elizabeth, and a son, Joseph. From architectural and landscape descriptions we felt that they probably lived somewhere near Oxford, England.

Another case was of a near-illiterate warrior who grunted a lot, but described being tired of fighting. He thought the king was, or had been called Edgar. He lived in a hut and appeared very poor, wearing a type of sacking material. His wife had died in childbirth and the baby shortly afterwards, which made the client under hypnosis cry. When asked to describe the happiest moment of his life, he described his death, when he said he was at peace. His body lay, arms folded across his chest, in a small open boat.

Even certain names, popular at a particular period in history helped me to verify whether the information was accurate: Edgar was certainly a Saxon king, and just prior to his reign there was a lot of Viking activity in England.

I recorded the life of a young woman who was married to a wealthy gentleman; they had a horse-drawn carriage and she described herself as wearing a bonnet as she looked at her reflection in an ornate mirror. She had four children, and these names rolled off her tongue like she had been using them her entire life.

I had a young man who was a sailor, and visited various islands; he was a bit of a rogue and carried illegal cargo. He was finally caught near the end of his lifetime and was hung for his deeds.

I experienced a regression as a young lady who might be described as a lady of the night! It certainly seemed that way at the beginning of the session. My sister Dianne, who is a qualified hypnotherapist, was taking me through this lifetime, and it made her nervous for me. It was dark at the start of this regression and I was down at the wharves. I wore a long dress and a cloak with a hood. Barges were being loaded by lantern light, and men were giving directions to crew. I remember stone arches where I hid myself among the shadows. I was quite comfortable and didn't feel nervous for myself. However, Dianne decided to move me out of this lifetime, so I was not able to gather any conclusions. Perhaps I will go back to that one some day and discover more . . .

A Universal Plan

Jacky: We loved learning about past lives and one of the most fascinating aspects was how we recognised characters from these previous lifetimes – people living with us today.

As sisters, we reincarnated together over and over again, in different roles for different 'plays'. In one, we were sisters, in others friends and sometimes parents and partners. Other family members appeared too. Was this the reason we were so close as a family in *this* life? Because we'd been together so many times before?

All the reincarnation research we had undertaken made me consider: were Dad's life-threatening conditions all part of a bigger life plan? Had they been agreed in advance? Was his soul perhaps assisting us on *our own* spiritual growth? It helped to feel the trauma had a purpose.

But what had been revealed from lessons in the past, or indeed past lives? What had we brought forward into the future? Did I feel stronger as a human soul, better able to cope as life threw up uncertainties? I felt that I *was* stronger.

And what had I discovered about the precious love a family can bring and the precarious walk we take between life and death? Love now, do it now, live it now; I'd certainly learned that, at least.

But would there be more challenges to come?

Chapter 7

The last challenge

The greatest glory in living lies not in
never falling, but in rising every time
we fall.

Nelson Mandela

Jacky and Madeline: After the months of trauma with Dad's brain tumour, he alternated between being extraordinarily well and very seriously ill. The next seven years brought many trials with them, including gallstones, a stroke and cancer. Debbie even joked that Dad should write a book called *The Good Hospital Guide*. He certainly seemed to be testing as many as possible for research!

A Warning from Heaven

Jacky: Dad was well enough at one point to travel to Spain. Eight of us went: Mum and Dad, my husband John and myself, our two daughters and my sister Di and her husband Dave. Mum and Dad had a time-share ownership of a villa and each year various family members would join them.

At the beginning of the holiday, Dad was exceptionally well, and one evening, we walked to a nearby hotel where there was live music each night. Dad tapped out the beat with his foot as the music played. Then he stood up and held out his hand to me, steady on his feet and ready to dance a 'quickstep'. Dad hadn't lost his touch and all eyes were watching us. I felt like a ballerina, as light as air. Then Dad ended the dance with his customary bow. It was magical.

But at the end of the week, Eric appeared to me in another dream. This time he came with a warning.

When I woke up, it took me a moment to orientate myself. I was lying in my white-walled bedroom in the villa.

Over breakfast that morning, when Mum and I were alone, I shared my strange dream with her. 'Eric came to visit me last night,' I told her.

'In one of your dreams? What did he say?'

'Well, he looked worried. He didn't say much actually, but seemed to be warning me.'

'About?' Mum asked, warily.

'Well, he seemed to be advising Dad against having any more operations.'

'Don't worry,' Mum reassured me. 'He's not due any operations; perhaps it was *just* a dream?'

'It didn't *feel* like a normal dream. It felt like when he visited before; it felt *real*.'

I suppressed my anxiety, but stayed alert.

That night, over dinner, Dad began to sweat and feel faint. Within an hour he was so unwell he went to bed. At six in the morning, Mum called us. Briefly, there was that feeling of déjà vu as Dad was rushed to hospital once again. Eric's dream warning was still ringing in my head. Here, no one could speak English, and we certainly didn't speak any Spanish. Silently, I began to pray for God, Eric, our guardian angels – or *anyone*'s angels – to help us.

Suddenly, a man walked over and spoke to us in perfect English: 'I couldn't help overhearing you. I'm a patient here myself. I speak fluent Spanish. Can I help?'

What a relief! The man acted as our interpreter, sharing our concerns with the medical staff. We then introduced our interpreter to Dad. We called him 'Our Guardian Angel'.

'I believe in Angels, actually,' our interpreter announced. And he pulled out a pendant that had been hanging round his neck; it featured two guardian angels. A strange coincidence? Or perhaps he was led to us, after all.

The doctor wanted to do an exploratory operation and I immediately felt a surge of panic. Operation? What should we do? Dianne and I were terrified and rang our sisters in the UK for advice.

'Follow your instincts and whatever you decide is OK with us,' they answered.

'We want to bring him home,' I said, remembering Eric's warning.

'Then do so,' was their brave reply.

Mum agreed. Her own mother, was warned in dreams that her son Billy could drown, and that was what had happened. Mum lost her big brother that day; she wasn't about to lose her husband too. Mum was now listening; if our family was somehow able to pick up warning messages from the other side, then surely we must pay attention.

The one and only English speaking doctor now called at the hospital on his day off – again, 'coincidentally'. We explained that we wanted to take Dad home to England and he eventually relented, to our enormous relief.

I marvelled that I'd *prayed* for some 'help' and it had immediately arrived. Eric and the gang had come through for us, but we still had much to do.

We were due to fly home in about five hours. Dad looked terrible. He was jaundiced and dehydrated. There was literally *just* enough time to catch the flight if we left for the airport immediately. We were determined to catch that flight – and we did.

Deep down, we knew we were doing the right thing. Uncle Eric might be dead, but my dream had been so vivid we felt compelled to heed his warning; and anyway, Dad wanted to go home too.

As soon as we touched down in England we took Dad straight to the local hospital. Doctors said Dad had floating gallstones. An 'exploratory operation' suggested by the Spanish surgeons would have been dangerous and quite unnecessary, they told us. In the end, Dad had a simple procedure and began to recover immediately.

I smiled in wonder at the resilience of this very exceptional man, and later thanked Eric for the warning. We still had Dad on our side of life for just a little longer.

Madeline: These events were so far beyond coincidence. It was just a question of being 'open' to the messages, *really* listening and having the confidence to act, not only on personal instinct, but on information suggested by the 'other side'.

A Dream Premonition

Jacky: One night, three weeks before Mum and Dad's golden wedding anniversary in the summer of 2004, I woke up from a horrible dream.

I'd been sitting across from a church, looking out of a window. Crowds of family and friends were arriving for a celebration, but I was unable to attend as I was somehow 'stuck' in this room.

Next, I saw a car arrive and Mum stepped out in her wedding dress. She looked young, the way she did as a bride of nineteen. Then Dad walked out of the church and escorted her down the aisle, a variation on the traditional wedding sequence. Other family members then followed them into the church to watch the wedding.

When I awoke I was desperately upset. How come so many other people could be at Mum and Dad's wedding party and I was unable to go? Then I remembered – it *was* only a dream.

But then three weeks later, on the weekend of the big wedding anniversary, I awoke in the night with raging toothache. John brought me a couple of the strongest painkillers he could find. The pain subsided, but only a little and I was banging my head against my hands in frustration. We called on the emergency doctors to ask for advice and I eventually ended up in the local hospital. They gave me an injection, but I needed to get to a dentist, and it was still too early in the morning to contact one (my own dentist was on holiday – another disaster). At one point, I accidentally took more medication than I should have, but this at least meant that for two hours I managed to get some sleep.

People had travelled long distances to attend Mum and Dad's celebration. I got up, washed and dressed, praying for assistance from 'anyone out there'. As we sat down for lunch with the family, I was indeed pain-free for nearly two hours. Bizarrely, in a photograph taken of John and me that day, I appear to have a glow around my head. No one would guess that I'd just had two hours sleep the night before.

Almost immediately after lunch John leaned over and asked kindly, 'Do you want to go home?' He had noticed my face turn pale as twinges started again. I agreed, and as we walked outside into the cold air, a stab of pain hit my mouth so strongly that I cried out in shock, tears pouring down my face.

It was at that moment I remembered my strange dream. Was it the wedding anniversary and not a wedding I was being warned about? *Someone* somewhere had managed to secure me a small window of time to join in on this most important of occasions before I had to leave and go home to bed.

Two days later, the tooth was removed, complete with abscess. I silently thanked my healers in the 'other realms' for all their help. I felt like the higher powers were saying, 'We can't stop the process, but we can delay it a little.' Those two hours were precious indeed.

Death in a Past Life

Madeline: I continued with my fascinating studies on reincarnation. My guided meditations included trips back into my own past lives. On one occasion, I was in ancient Rome where, unfortunately, I was thrown to the lions in a large arena. As I lifted above the scene, I felt no pain or emotion relating to what I was seeing. I was later laid out on a pallet and died of my wounds.

One person wept for me, trying to tend my bleeding and

battered body. It was Mum! She was a young woman dressed in black. I knew she was a relative of mine in this other life too. It didn't look like her, of course, but on a soul level I recognised her. I had no points of reference for the scene I was witnessing. I didn't know whether it was historically accurate or not. I looked at my sandals tied up to my knees; my ripped and dirty tunic and I remembered the cold touch of marble and stone of the walls. It felt like a memory.

During another past life, I was a young Native American Indian girl and I lived with my grandmother, who had bad and missing teeth. Where do these lives surface from? Does something that happens in our current lifetime prompt us to recall (under hypnosis or dreams) specific lifetimes? Maybe they were to help us to learn a lesson in this lifetime? No wonder we were meant to forget – it was hard enough concentrating on the one we were living now!

Past-life Castration

Jacky: One night, when we were staying at my sister-in-law Jill's house, I had a strange experience. Midway through a boring dream, the scene slid to one side and a new vision came into view. Immediately, I was fully lucid, aware and 'awake', while my body slept on.

Below me was a panoramic view of a scene – a past life. I was both watching the vision from above and taking part, all at the same time. I was kneeling down in front of the mistress of the house and I was one of a 'matching pair' of eunuchs. In reality I wasn't even sure what the word meant and yet I was hearing it now. I was in a room decorated with beautifully draped fabrics; my mistress was dressed in fine clothes and jewellery. She held a royal rank. Another servant had betrayed me – I was getting the blame for something that *he* had done. My fate was to be beheaded.

When I awoke, I sat momentarily stunned. What was that? I wondered. But I knew it wasn't a dream, I was recalling a past life. I remember then creeping around in the darkness of my sister-in-law's house, even going downstairs, so that I could find a pen and paper to write it down. I *had* to remember this.

Several years later, I was answering 'interview' questions via email for a magazine. One of the questions was: 'What is the strangest paranormal experience you've ever had?' This vision came to mind, so I went on to the internet and confirmed the definition: 'Eunuch' is a term which refers to castrated males. They were 'created' to perform specific social functions (common in past societies). Castration was regularly done to domestic servants especially those who worked with women. They were considered 'safer' servants, particularly in royal courts. Servants, my reference stated, could easily be killed without repercussions. Strangely, my research seemed to validate my dream.

Warning From Dad's Spirit

Madeline and I weren't the only one having strange experiences. Following Dad's last illness, Dianne had woken up once in the middle of the night. In the bathroom, she'd caught a strange reflection in the mirror. After a double take, she'd realised it *was* Dad. She saw his faint, almost spooky manifestation reflected back at her. But he was alive wasn't he? In her head she asked him, 'What are you doing here?' He told her, 'You've got to get used to seeing me like this . . . '

Dianne was worried; if she'd seen Dad in the mirror, did it mean he'd died? After investigation, she discovered, to her relief, that Dad was fine and at home, asleep in bed. But did his spirit know something that we did not?

In my files, I have cases where the souls of those still living appear to loved ones to say goodbye in the days and weeks before passing over to the other side of life. When Dianne told me about her experience, I was concerned. Why *was* Dianne going to have to get used to seeing Dad in the mirror? Something wasn't right. And although Dad was alive and seemed well, we soon discovered that all was not as it seemed.

Madeline: The next day, Dad was fishing down at the river-bank with a friend when he collapsed with a stroke. He was taken to hospital, and the medical staff on the stroke ward were brilliant, kind and efficient. Dad was in good hands.

But I recalled Dianne's late-night vision in the mirror: 'You've got to get used to seeing me like this . . . ' Somebody knew what was going on and what was going to happen. Maybe even a 'higher' part of Dad himself?

More Life Lessons

Jacky: I wondered now, as I'd wondered before: are the main parts of our lives mapped out in advance? Was every illness and tragedy just another lesson in the classroom, a lesson called 'life on Earth'? Dad's illnesses had taught us so much: that family comes first; that love is the most important lesson of all – nothing matters more than that. I remembered Madeline saying,

'Look how we've all pulled together; become a closer family ... there's a reason for everything, even if we aren't always aware of it right away.'

Dad had a gorgeous blue sweater that worked beautifully with his skin tone, making him look well and healthy. We insisted he wear it in hospital and he got plenty of compliments from the kind nursing staff. Dad, in his turn, thrived on the praise and made an excellent recovery.

Too Much

Madeline: 'Happy birthday, Dad!' It was September 2007 and Dad was seventy-seven years old. He looked fantastic – lean and fit, tanned after the summer and wearing one of his flattering blue tops.

So when we visited the following month, we were surprised to discover there were yet more problems. Dad had been diagnosed with cancer of the tongue, brought on by years of smoking cigarettes.

Jacky: I cried on the phone to Debbie. 'I can't do this any more,' I said. 'I just can't keep doing this.' The constant visits to hospital, Dad teetering on the edge of life, so many years of suffering. I felt guilty. Was I sorry for Dad or for myself though? I realised it was probably both.

Debbie and Dianne admitted to crying with despair too. How much more can one man put up with, we all wondered. But wishing away the pain wasn't going to help. And so we carried on as normal, caring for the man we adored.

Madeline: I arrived in the Midlands late on Sunday and, again, Dad looked so well. But on Monday morning he was pessimistic about his 'odds'.

'Well, I've got away with a lot, but this time it's *got* me,' he said, dejectedly.

'What do you mean?' I asked, dubiously.

'Well, cancer. I mean, it's the 'big one', isn't it?' he sounded beaten.

'Dad, I know you were in a coma for most of the time, but have you any idea what you've come through already?'

'What do you mean?' Dad raised his eyes and looked at me.

I was convinced this illness wouldn't be anywhere near as challenging as anything we'd already been through with him, and told him so: 'If you can get through a brain tumour which took six operations to get right, then meningitis, two collapsed lungs, a tracheotomy, a broken pelvis, gallstones *and* a stroke, then I'm damned sure you can battle a few cancer cells!' I knew I sounded bossy, but I was trying to reassure him, to remind him of all the things he had survived. He could beat this.

The Choice to 'Stay' or Go

Jacky: That night I had another dream visitation. This time Uncle Eric told me: 'Dad has finished all his challenges for this life. He can come to us when he's ready, or stay longer on Earth if he wants to.' He was very matter of fact about it.

In my dream, I was shown that this was *the best* Dad's health was going to be from now on. Good food and exercise would no longer lengthen his life. Life would now be a gradual deterioration – a downhill journey from this point on.

It was hard to decide whether to feel depressed or elated for Dad. It was clear that what happened next was totally up to him. He could stay, and suffer with a failing body, or go to heaven and join his loving family on the other side of life. It was his choice.

Eric gave me a time span for the remainder of Dad's life – around three to eighteen months more. I was frightened, but didn't want to give anyone else the timescale. Does anyone want to know *when* they're going to die? In the end, however, I *did* tell John. I had to share it with someone. I was sad, knowing what I knew, but at the same time relieved to have had this 'heavenly' advance warning. I had time to prepare myself . . .

Surprisingly, Dad made it through the ten-hour operation, but I couldn't help wondering, should we have encouraged him to go through with it this time? He was dying, one small bit at a time.

The Last Time

Madeline: We visited Dad late that evening. Dad's body was getting tired and as his son-in-law, Nick, looked into his eyes he held his hand. Dad's eyes were teary, and Nick felt guilty and distressed and wanted to convey his innermost feelings. They held each other's gaze and Nick sensed that he'd made a silent connection with Dad. His unspoken thoughts were: You don't have to do this any more, Ron. It's OK, we understand. You've been through so much and we keep holding on to you, willing you to survive against the odds. Let's make this the last time. You don't have to keep going through these terrible operations and illnesses.

That night, Nick was of the opinion, that he would rather let Dad go, with love, than watch him suffer any more.

But it wasn't over yet.

Meeting on the Astral Plane

It was the end of November, and the morning of my birthday. Dad was back on the ward. As we left the hospital for home, Mum asked Dad if he'd wished me a happy birthday. He duly picked up a pad of paper and wrote:

> Happy birthday to my darling Baby Daughter,
> All my best wishes from Daddy x x x x x x x x x x

I still have that piece of lined paper, torn from the notepad. Sentimentally, I kept it – just in case it was the last thing he ever wrote to me. It was.

Jacky: Why does he have to suffer? I asked myself. Why? As I went to bed, I looked heavenwards. Please let me be with Dad tonight, I begged, imagining myself sitting beside him in the hospital, holding his hand. Surprisingly, I went straight to sleep, and although I don't remember another thing about it, I felt sure that I had fixed it so that I *was* with Dad on some level. I certainly hoped so.

The next day was Madeline's birthday. We went for dinner together. We chatted about how we felt about Dad – the sadness, the despair. During the meal, I shared with Madeline my wish of the previous evening to spend the night by Dad's bedside. Then my mobile rang with a text message from Debbie.

She told me she'd had a visit from Eric in the night; she said it was awesome.

Later, Debbie shared her experience with everybody. She too had longed to sit with Dad during the night, and she was luckier than me, as our dearest Uncle Eric had appeared to her in a dream.

'Is Dad OK?' Debbie had asked Eric.

'Yes,' he told her.

'Can I see him?'

'Yes,' he said. 'Come with me.' And Eric took Debbie's hand and they lifted off the bed. They were flying, out of body! It sounds quite bizarre, but they were in long, white, flowing cotton night gowns (not Debbie's usual bedroom attire) flying, like Peter Pan and Wendy down the dual carriageway in the direction of the hospital. This was Debbie's first attempt at astral projection and she told us it took ages; they were flying really slowly. She remembered landmarks en route – a café, trees and a roundabout.

Finally, Debbie and Eric reached Dad's hospital ward. Dad was sleeping peacefully, but to Debbie's surprise, I'd arrived before her! There I was, hovering above his bed, dressed in my normal day wear. Debbie remembered feeling slightly peeved because, *apparently*, I'd beaten her to it; already out of body and at the hospital with Dad.

Madeline: Debbie described looking around the intensive-care room which looked exactly as it had a few hours earlier except that there were lots of spirit people there too. She recognised some of them: Mum's parents, Dad's father (she knew him from photographs she'd seen), Dad's stepfather, and Dad's mum, May.

There were lots more people in the room, she told us – too many for her to pick out individually, and some she didn't know, in any case. And then it dawned on her: the one thing they had in common – they were all dead (apart from Jacky). They were standing looking at our sleeping father and chatting excitedly. Debbie described the whole experience as overwhelmingly thrilling, and considered for a moment just how much petrol and parking money she could save if she did this every day!

The next thing she remembered was waking up in her own bed and thinking, 'I can't wait to tell everyone.'

Jacky: Debbie was a little disappointed that I had no recollection of our meeting on the 'astral plane', but sadly, all I remembered was my original request before I fell into a deep sleep that night. I had *asked* if I could be with Dad and, apparently, I was. My spirit seems to be way more advanced than I am.

But this wasn't the first time something like this had happened to me. Once, my mother was taking care of a very sick friend, and I'd visited her during the day. When I left, I asked the angels to visit *her* and, sure enough, she'd woken in the night to see her room full of angels. She actually *saw me* in the room too, sitting in the corner. She said I appeared to be orchestrating the angels somehow, and she felt that they were there at my request. In the morning she chastised me, joking that they'd disturbed her with their loud singing. She felt sure I would remember. But as with Debbie's experience, I remembered nothing at all!

I think it just goes to show, intent is everything: know it, believe it and it will be so.

One Last Christmas

Madeline: We'd done it! We'd managed to arrive at another Christmas, and we'd kept Dad alive *again* to celebrate it with us. How this man continued to survive amazed me. He looked a little battle weary this time, from his difficult struggle with cancer, but seemed determined to stay with us all, as long as his body kept up the fight.

Dad cried when he opened his Christmas card. Tucked inside were two tickets to see the London show, *Joseph and the Amazing Technicolor Dreamcoat*. Dad had mentioned many times that he would love to see the musical; we didn't quite expect the emotional response that we got though, and we were really touched at how thrilled he was. We'd all clubbed together to buy the gift – a mini break for Mum and Dad in London, incorporating the show and a hotel and, as we knew Dad wouldn't be able to drive there, travel down to London by coach.

The date for the trip was in February. We often felt like we'd kept Dad on borrowed time since his brain tumour nine years earlier. But now I wondered if he had enough time left . . .

A Final 'Date'

Jacky: We'd reached February. And it was the day of the Joseph trip.

After depositing their bags at the hotel, Mum and Dad were picked up by coach and dropped close to the theatre with plenty of time for a meal before the show.

Mum told us that Dad had felt cold – the significance of

which was not clear to us until a few days later. Yet he was excited as Mum suggested they have a glass of sherry before they ate – 'to warm him up'. They had a delicious meal, after which the two of them had a liqueur and a coffee, a rare treat. The show was amazing – everything Dad had expected and more.

But when they got back to the hotel, Dad was still cold and found it hard to sleep in the hotel's single bed, being used to snuggling close to his wife of fifty-three years.

It was a very special weekend for Mum and Dad and, as it turned out, their last weekend away together. We didn't know it at the time, but Dad was cold because he was going into heart failure.

Dad died one week later.

PART III

Dad Had Died ... but He Certainly Wasn't Dead

Chapter 8

Time gentlemen, please

I am ready to meet my Maker. Whether
my Maker is prepared for the great ordeal
of meeting me is another matter.

Winston Churchill

Michael's Back with 'Dad's Song'

Madeline: On the night Dad died, we sat chatting, crying
and smiling at memories late into the night. When I finally
fell into bed, I was exhausted, but too sad to sleep. I
picked up my new book and was briefly caught up in the
story. About half an hour later, I was ready to switch off the
light.

With the story still on my mind I drifted off to sleep, but the
soft strains of Michael Bublé singing, 'I've Got the World on a
String' began playing in my head, like my own private concert.
The song played over and over again. It felt like Dad really was
sitting on that rainbow, pondering on his wonderful life,

despite his many illnesses, and reminding me how much he'd enjoyed sharing that life with his family.

Surprisingly, I slept for five hours that night. Yet, as I surfaced, the song was right there, still playing in my head. This was the beginning of a mystery.

' . . . Got the World on a String'

Jacky: The new apartment that Mum and Dad had hoped to share was extremely small compared to the ten-room bungalow they'd just sold, after fourteen years living there.

Luckily, we sisters had already begun clearing and sorting through their many years' worth of belongings, to reduce them to a more manageable quantity for their new life.

'Which of these ties do you want to keep, Dad?' we'd asked him, lining them all up on the floor for him, so he could choose his favourites. There were piles of collared shirts too, and Dad had insisted on keeping so many of them.

We'd done the same thing with Mum, who although reluctant at first, had soon begun to enjoy the process. I'd emptied cupboards full of crockery so she could choose: ten vases, fifteen jugs, over a hundred mugs and ten tea sets – all collected over a lifetime. 'Only keep the gorgeous things and the things you love.' Debbie had advised, and this had really helped.

But what started out a challenge and a trauma had soon become fun and exciting. I'd been so proud of them both for entering into the spirit of things, with Dad laughingly telling us, 'Throw it all out, I don't mind!'

I thought now of the wardrobe full of clothes that we'd gone through just a couple of weeks before – clothes that would never again be worn. Still, looking back over the clearing out we'd done together, I realised how it would help now. Much of the work had already been accomplished and Dad had discarded many of the things he no longer wanted.

Dad left us right after the sale of the house and before the move. We had a funeral to arrange and it would fit neatly in the middle, giving us the opportunity to hold a final farewell party in his honour in the bungalow he had loved. Dad's timing – if there ever is such a thing – was perfect down to the last detail!

As I climbed the stairs now to bed, it occurred to me that I probably wouldn't sleep, but as my head hit the pillow I heard Michael Bublé singing, 'I've Got the World on a String', somewhere in the back of my mind.

Goodnight Dad, I thought. *Sleep tight . . .*

Dad Visits 'His Girls'

The following morning, we all gathered at Mum's and fell into each other's arms. We were still in shock, but gained comfort from being together. We sat in the breakfast room at the bungalow. Dad was gone . . . but we each held a 'secret' and, one by one, we began to reveal them. Debbie went first.

Dad showed what happened when he died

During the night Debbie dreamed that she was in the hospital with Dad. She told us she'd felt aware and lucid and was completely conscious of the fact that she was asleep, so this was less like an ordinary dream than a real face-to-face conversation.

In the 'dream', Dad was sitting on a hospital chair. He was flicking through piles and piles of greeting cards and appeared overwhelmed and grateful that so many people cared enough to send them.

'But Dad didn't have any cards in hospital did he?' asked Dianne.

'No,' said Debbie. 'That's exactly what I thought; in fact, I felt he was trying to explain something to me, but wasn't sure what he meant.'

Less than a week later, over 140 'sympathy' cards arrived. It seemed almost as if Dad had glimpsed the cards and messages of love ahead of time. He appeared to be showing Debbie this, in his visit from the afterlife. Dad also showed Debbie exactly what happened when he died.

'In my "dream",' she told us, 'Dad grabbed his chest. I felt he was showing me he only had one pain in his heart.' She described how, after a brief moment of distress, it had stopped, and pain-free, his spirit had begun to sit up and separate from his physical body which was still lying on the bed, before floating towards the ceiling. In Debbie's night-time vision, the paramedics had come rushing in to restart Dad's heart, but Debbie put up her hand to stop them, to bar their way. She shook her head, as if denying permission for them to try and restart the heart in his frail body. Of course, in real life, we weren't even there at his moment of passing, but we all agreed with the sentiment. Dad had been ready to leave his body and we all knew it.

Was Dad now showing Debbie he knew it was OK to leave us? Had *we*, on some higher spiritual level, given permission for our beloved Dad to leave his worn out and tired body, the body that had caused him so much pain in life?

It seemed simple: he hadn't suffered and death was easy – this was the message. He was trying to reassure Debbie, knowing she'd share the experience with her sisters and with Mum, who was wandering in and out of the room as we chatted, picking up fragments of our conversation.

'Dad was now lying on the floor, in my dream,' Debbie continued. 'That blue towel was rolled under his head like a pillow. He was alive! Alive in the dream, anyway; and maybe *alive* in another dimension.'

Before leaving the dream visit Dad gave Debbie one more insight:

'He had people around him and seemed really happy.' Debbie described Dad surrounded by hordes of deceased family and friends. Dad was going home, with a welcoming committee there to greet him.

The welcome party

Dad had been busy, and it was now time to reveal *my* 'secret', which I'd already discussed with John over breakfast.

'Guess what?' I exclaimed to my sisters. 'I saw Dad last night too.' Dianne and Madeline exchanged knowing smiles. 'In fact, part of my dream sounds a bit like yours Deb,' I continued. 'Dad was excited, and I also saw him surrounded by crowds of people who'd come to greet him. But in *my* dream, he was rushing to shake hands with queues of family and friends who were lining up in front of him.'

'Really?' Debbie seemed amazed.

'Yes, honestly; he kept holding up his hand to his head, as if in surprise, saying, "I can't believe it, I can't believe you're all here!"'

As in Debbie's dream, Dad had seemed overjoyed and thrilled.

Funeral prediction

Madeline: When Jacky had finished, I glanced at Dianne, who nodded, indicating that I should go next; we'd discussed our own 'visits' from Dad before the others had arrived.

'Funnily enough,' I said, smiling, 'I too had a Dad experience last night.' Jacky and Debbie turned to me, expectantly.

My experience had been very lucid and clear too. 'Dad looked really well, exactly as he'd looked about six months ago,' I explained, eagerly. 'He had his walking stick and was sitting forward, leaning on it, like in that lovely photograph you took of him.' I said to Jacky. This was a favourite shot of Dad where he looked relaxed and contented. 'He was talking about his funeral.'

'What do you mean?'

'It was like he knew about it; he seemed overcome with emotion at the thought of his funeral, and shook his head in astonishment saying, "I can't believe how many people have come to my funeral." He was so touched.'

The 'dream' felt like a real visit from Dad, as if he was trying to give me a message. At this stage, we hadn't really discussed the funeral arrangements, apart from the one song. We were still in the early process of letting people know that he'd died. As the week went on, it became clear that the funeral was going to be very well attended, just as Dad 'predicted'.

But Dad had talked about another event that hadn't happened yet. He was showing me that 'time' is only relevant to those of us on 'this side' of life. I went on:

'In the next part of the dream, Dad became younger – he was about forty, I'd guess. I was sitting and he walked over to me.' I paused as I remembered how excited I'd felt at this moment during my night-time visit. 'Dad held out his hands, I took hold of them and stood up, and he guided me round the floor, we danced a quickstep together.'

I could only dance a quickstep with Dad, because I wasn't good enough with any other dance partner. But Dad was an expert and steered me around effortlessly. It was the best 'last dance' a girl could have with her Dad – an amazing experience. I then recalled the last time I'd danced with Dad when he was alive and shared it with the others.

'It was three years ago,' I said, 'when we took Mum and Dad to that dinner-dance in Cornwall. Dad was a little unsteady on his legs, but he wasn't yet using his stick,' I reminisced. My sisters smiled, and Mum came in and perched on the edge of a chair. 'He held me on the dance floor with the lightest of touches, just with his fingertips really, but his direction was so strong, that I stayed in step. He even added a little flourish in the corner of the dance floor and flung me out to one side dramatically, like a professional dancer.' I demonstrated this with some hand movements.

'Like he always did,' Jacky remembered. The others nodded in agreement.

'We danced a quickstep together early in the evening and had the wooden dance floor all to ourselves,' I said.

Then Mum joined in the conversation, saying, 'When you left the floor, you got a round of applause from the other guests, I remember. Your dad loved that.' She smiled sadly.

Dancing was an important part of Dad's life, and it was something we had shared with him since we were little girls. Through his dream visit, Dad was reminding me of our connection in life, apparently unbroken by death.

Jacky: Mum stood up. 'I've just put the kettle on,' she said. 'Does anyone want a drink?'

'Yes, lovely.' Dianne shuffled in her chair. 'But let me tell you about *my* dream first.' Mum sat down again before Dianne continued.

'Unfortunately, I didn't get much sleep last night,' she explained. 'But it was worth it – because when I finally dropped off, Dad came to visit me too.'

A buzz of delight filled the room.

Dianne's reunion with Dad was brief, she explained. 'Dad was just passing through – like he was on his way somewhere. He was with Uncle Eric. They both seemed so happy and were waving at me. I could feel their energy. They were both so vibrant – almost energetic – and it was like their energy was all around me. Then they seemed to fade away.'

We were all thrilled; this wasn't how we'd expected to feel today. We hugged each other again. Instead of grief, we all had a feeling of optimistic relief. Mum got up now to make some tea, while the rest of us continued with our jobs sorting the house, a feeling of comfort upon us.

Holiday fun from the other side

The second night after Dad died, I had another dream 'visit' from him.

That day, I'd been chatting to my poor daughter Charlotte, who was struggling to come to terms with her granddad's death. I suggested that she try and imagine her granddad was on an extended holiday. And my dream that night seemed to imply that Dad had been listening in on our conversation!

As soon as I closed my eyes, I heard giggling. Dad was lying on a deckchair. He was young and bronzed with big muscles.

Bizarrely, he was wearing a sombrero hat and drinking a large cocktail out of half a pineapple. It was then that I discovered the giggler. Sitting next to Dad, also on a deckchair was his brother Eric. Eric's body was young and bronzed too, but he appeared with an older head; he was greying and nearly bald, just as I'd known him in life. Perhaps they believed I might not recognise a 'young' Uncle Eric? In any event, they were having enormous fun, like a couple of school children away from their parents and up to no good.

Next, I saw two large cars up on the beach. The expensive-looking 'heavenly' cars were theirs; then the dream vision changed, and I remember watching them dive into the sea before jumping aboard speedboats and whizzing round the bay. I actually woke up laughing! Here I was, less than three whole days since my father's death, and I was roaring with laugher, just as Dad would have done in life.

As before, the dream was powerful and real. This was no ordinary dream. Dad and Eric were using the sense of humour they'd had in life to show me how fit they were – swimming, as well as happily drinking exotic cocktails and even owning expensive cars. Dad could do everything he wanted in heaven – and maybe a few things he'd been unable to do in life too!

The next morning was taken up with phone calls to shocked family and friends, and in between we talked about Dad and his strange 'visits'. The visits seemed planned and relevant to special people in his life. Taken individually, they seemed funny 'coincidences', but viewed as a whole, they were hard to dismiss. And there was more . . .

Chapter 9

Gone fishing

The report of my death was greatly exaggerated.

Mark Twain

Doorbell Tricks ...

Madeline: Dad's very close friend Daphne rang Mum after hearing the sad news. As Mum answered the telephone, the doorbell rang at exactly the same moment with the usual single 'Eric ... or Dad?' chime. Nick jumped up to answer the door, but quickly came back smiling – as usual, 'nobody' was at the front door. Debbie and I gawped, open-mouthed at the timing. Daphne was a close family friend, and adored Dad. Speaking to Mum on the phone, she was naturally devastated. Dad would always have jumped up to greet his dear friend in life, and had, it seemed, discovered a new way to greet her from heaven.

. . . and Lightbulb Flickers

Later the same day, Mum received a distraught phone call from a local friend, Terry, one of Dad's closest pals and fishing mates. As Mum picked up the phone, the light in the dining room buzzed and flickered for about five seconds, then came back on again as brightly as before. Again, we looked at each other in amazement. Dad again? We knew it was!

There was always a pattern to the experiences. None was ever haphazard. Either the doorbell rang or the light flickered as we spoke about Dad or they did so when one of his favourite friends rang, or immediately before, as if announcing the call. The buzzing light bulb was particularly bizarre.

Another phone call the same day was from Jim, another old friend. As he announced his name to Mum, the light in the dining room started going crazy, flickering as if in excitement, before going out completely. We thought at first that the bulb had blown this time, and that this perhaps, disappointingly, explained why it had been flickering before. But then, just as suddenly, the light came back on again, as if to say, 'Ha ha, only joking.' And this time it remained steady, never to flicker again.

When we questioned a particular type of phenomenon or attempted to pass it off as 'coincidence', it would often stop, only to be replaced with different and new kinds of phenomena. It seemed at no point did 'they' want us to become complacent.

Dad Shows the Way

Mum decided she would still like to move to the smaller, luxury apartment as she and Dad had originally planned. But on the Thursday morning of the week Dad died, Mum had a major panic.

'I've been awake all night,' she told me. 'It was a lovely idea, but I've realised that without your dad, I can't afford to live there on my own.' She was pink-eyed, and had obviously being crying.

'What are you going to do? There must be some way,' I told her. 'Let's wait until we've looked at all your finances. We don't know yet; don't close your mind to it until we've explored every avenue.'

But Mum was adamant. 'Without your dad's pension, there is no way. Look, I've written down what I have coming in, and what my bills will be. There won't be enough money.' Mum showed me a small piece of torn cardboard, about half the size of a postcard, where she'd scrawled some figures.

I was equally adamant: 'Mum – you can't decide the rest of your life on the back of this scrap of tattered card! Please, let's wait,' I insisted. I quickly disappeared, and telephoned Jacky,

'Please come and help me,' I begged. 'Mum has decided she can't afford to move to the new apartment. I need John to look at her finances. This is so important.'

'Well, strangely enough, John hasn't actually left for work yet; he stayed home to meet our accountant this morning. Leave it with me. I'll see what I can do. And don't worry, I had another interesting dream visitation last night. Everything will be fine – Dad told me,' she said, confidently.

I telephoned Debbie and asked her to come round too – reinforcements. Dianne arrived moments later. We needed to work on a plan together. We talked about visiting the apartments – they were just around the corner; perhaps a smaller one would be available? Surely that would cost less money?

Jacky: Day three and Dad visited again in a dream. I barely had time to discuss it with John before our accountant arrived at the door and, during his visit, Madeline rang to request we call round to help with a financial 'crisis'. So as soon as our own meeting was over, we drove round there.

Someone made the inevitable cup of tea and I sat down to explain my 'dream' of the night before. While I was asleep, Dad had showed me a table full of objects. Each was a symbol of good news ahead; I realised this from the feeling he was sharing with me. Dad was trying to show me that he knew what was coming next in our lives and, as he pointed to the objects, he grinned and gave me his signature 'thumbs-up' sign.

On the table were his old wallet, bulging with cash, something that looked like a penknife and a car key.

A wallet full of cash: that had to mean Mum would be OK for money, right? Was Dad aware of Mum's sleepless night and trying to get a message of reassurance to her? I knew he was.

John would normally be at work, over an hour's drive away from the house. We'd already asked each other, 'Why have we arranged to meet with our accountant before work, like this?' Usually, we'd get together in the evening or over the weekend. But because of this strange decision, John was now available to help Mum. He took the rest of the day off work and several hours later, after he and Dianne trawled through Mum's paperwork, we realised there was much more money than she'd thought.

The others arrived back from the new retirement apartments with the news that Mum could downsize and save herself a considerable amount of cash. They'd found the ideal spot – a smaller single flat, close to the restaurant area where all the activity would be. Perfect for this sociable lady!

'We've reserved it for you Mum,' they told her. 'Do you want to go and look?'

But Mum just cried with relief. 'No, it's fine. I trust you,' she said.

Dad was certainly keeping an eye on things from the other side. As I updated the others about my dream, I remembered the penknife. 'Dad didn't have a penknife, did he?' I asked Mum.

Mum laughed for the first time that morning. 'Open the kitchen drawer,' she said.

'Oh yes. Here it is,' I said, recognising it immediately. 'This is what I saw in my dream.' I held it up, excitedly.

'Bring it in here,' Mum requested.

I handed it over. 'Look,' she said, opening it up. 'It's *not* a penknife!' Mum opened it to reveal a spiral corkscrew – it was a wine waiter's gadget, and the 'knife' part was for removing the foil on bottles of wine. Immediately, we got it – Dad was having a reunion party on the heavenly side and wanted us to have a one for him *here*. Now seemed the perfect time to celebrate Mum's new apartment and, a week later, at the funeral, we celebrated Dad's life, exactly as he'd requested – using the bottle opener, of course!

In the hustle and bustle, the car key in my dream was momentarily forgotten, but like everything else Dad showed us, we worked it out eventually . . .

A Real Visit

In the meantime, Dad was still busy visiting. On that same day his granddaughter Georgina was in the house on her own. She was walking across the landing at the top of the stairs at our house, when she suddenly became aware of a 'man' standing at the bottom. Georgina immediately let out a shocked scream, thinking someone had broken in. But when she looked again, her heart beating fast, the man didn't move. Then she noticed a familiar walking stick, and clearer details of the visitor appeared. It was Granddad – just popping in to say hello! He was standing there, large as life and clear as day, if not slightly deceased!

Georgina was relieved. A 'ghost' was better than a burglar. And she hadn't time to be afraid of encountering a spirit, because no sooner had she remembered Granddad had died, than the spirit vision faded away. Of course, she hastily rang to tell me, although I have to confess she was a little shaken up when she called.

Grandson's Visit

Madeline: It was 29 February, just four days since Dad's passing. There were still people we had to inform, we had a funeral to organise and a house move to arrange. We were sitting in the snug, drinking tea and making lists, when Sam, my mature thirteen-year-old son, wandered downstairs to share his early-morning encounter. He told us about the 'weird' dream he'd had that morning involving his Granddad. We all stopped what we were doing to listen.

'I had a dream about Granddad last night,' Sam began. 'I was sitting on the bed in the single room upstairs, and I was looking for Jim. For some reason, I checked behind the chest of drawers! The door was open and I could see Granddad on the landing. He just said, "All right, Sam?"'

'Did you answer?'

'Yes. I said, "All right, Granddad?" It was as if nothing had happened, but I knew he was dead. Then I went into Nan's room and I was lying on a single bed.'

In reality, our parents had a king-sized bed at the bungalow; this single bed did not exist in 'real' space and time. Not yet, anyway. Sam continued: 'The room looked different to their bedroom upstairs, but I *knew* that it was Nan's room.'

'What did it look like?' we asked.

'Well, the walls were painted cream and it was really brightly lit.'

'OK. What else do you remember?'

'I was watching a *Tintin* cartoon on a flat-screen TV, which was on the bedroom wall.'

'Oh yes, Granddad enjoyed *Tintin* too, didn't he?' I reflected; it was something the 'boys' all shared.

'The room was really bright; I don't know where the brightness was coming from. Then Granddad walked into the bedroom – he had his walking stick – and wandered around. Then he spoke to me again and said, "Hello, my darling," in a funny, deep voice. I said, "Hello Granddad." Then he wandered back out on to the landing and I woke up.'

Sam had no idea then that when his nan moved to her new apartment she would buy a single bed and sell the king-size divan she had shared with Dad. Mum also later sold her old-fashioned television sets, planning to replace them with brand new flat screens, including one for the bedroom. Also, the new bedroom walls are painted cream, while the window overlooks a courtyard garden that is brightly lit all night long. All exactly as Sam had seen.

As always, Dad seemed to be showing that he knew what was happening next in his family's life.

Sam took his dream visit totally in his stride. He said it felt 'real' and it didn't upset or disturb him in any way. Quite the opposite, in fact; Sam felt comforted by the fact that Granddad still seemed to be 'around'.

Keeping our Spirits Up

Jacky: Later the same day, the funeral director came to call, so that we could discuss final details for the service. As usual, the 'girls' gathered in the snug with Mum, the small space being the most intimate for chatting.

'Is there anything you'd like to put in the coffin?' the funeral director asked kindly. 'People often tuck a packet of cigarettes in the coffin, for example.'

'Cigarettes?' we chorused. 'No way!'

'What about a packet of mints though?' someone suggested. 'He always had a packet of mints in his pocket.'

'Yes – and indigestion tablets!' We were all laughing now.

'What about his Masonic ritual book . . . a fishing reel .. . his driving licence?' On a roll now, we joked around for a few minutes more coming up with more and more outrageous suggestions before the funeral director brought us back to the job in hand.

'Well, you can have a think about it for a few days,' she said. 'And if you want to add anything, get it over to me the day before the funeral.'

We had big plans for the service and talked about this next.

'So, it's agreed then: we arrange most of the funeral ourselves, yes?'

'Yes, of course. I have the perfect person to conduct the service for you,' she said, smiling kindly. 'You're looking for more of a humanist service? Less religious?'

'Well, Dad was certainly more spiritual than religious,' we agreed.

Right on cue, the moment we mentioned Dad's name, the doorbell rang its usual single ring to indicate a 'spirit visitor'.

The funeral director looked surprised when we ignored it. 'Erm . . . did I hear the doorbell?' she asked. I'm sure she felt we must all be too distressed in our grief to hear the chime. We explained about the timely ringing, but I went to the door to check – just in case. Of course, as usual, no one was there.

And so it went on. We learned that it's possible to laugh and enjoy the world around you, even in the week your father passes away. Dad seemed determined to keep our 'spirits' up.

Lighting the Way

Madeline: The funeral was planned for 6 March. Debbie's birthday was on the fourth, and John suggested that as I was up from Cornwall, the girls should take the opportunity to go out for lunch together, and have a few hours off from the funeral arrangements, just Mum and daughters. Looking back, I can't remember that we'd ever done this before – it was an ideal opportunity.

Jacky drove us to a pretty French-style crêperie where we persuaded the staff to open the quiet upstairs area for us. The five of us sat at a large, round wooden table in the low-lit empty room. We agreed not to talk about the funeral, but to celebrate Debbie's birthday instead.

We ordered our meals and chatted for a while. Then I noticed a dramatic shaft of sunlight streaming through the skylight. The beam was intense; it angled across the room and landed in a large, brilliant splash of sunshine underneath

Mum's chair. It was breathtaking. We all gasped in delight and, as usual, Dad got the 'blame'. Jacky tried to take a photograph of it, but couldn't work out how to turn off the flash, so the light from her camera flooded the area with brightness, effectively wiping out the clear and straight line of radiance we had all so clearly witnessed with our own eyes.

A Fun Experience

The day before the funeral, we went to the supermarket to buy the fresh food. Sam was left in charge of younger brother Jim, and the boys knew they could ring if they needed anything. We would only be an hour.

While we were out, Jim was playing with his toy rabbit in the lounge at the bungalow and threw it up into the air and on to Granddad's chair. Just a day before, Jacky had sat in it and tried to get the footstool out – you had to push down *hard* on the arms of the chair and lean backwards at the same time to make it pop out from underneath – but it was really stiff and rusted. Yet, as Jim's toy rabbit – a long, skinny, light-weight thing – landed on the chair, the footstool flew out immediately.

The boys realised this was unusual and were very excited. Right away, they wondered if Granddad was up to his usual tricks, especially as it was *his* chair. Eagerly, they rang us on the mobile phone to share their experience.

Later, Madeline asked Sam if he'd actually witnessed it. 'Oh yes!' he said, and told her it was a fun experience and not a bit scary.

The 'subtle' little signs seemed to be growing in number.

Dad Makes His Presence Felt

Jacky: Before Dad's passing, Dianne had booked an appointment with her manicurist, Sarah, and she decided now to go ahead with it. She wanted her nails to be tidy for the funeral the following day.

Sarah and Dianne chatted about the events of the week: light bulbs flickering, the doorbell, alarm clocks going off and so on. Dianne explained to Sarah how she kept feeling a cold shiver, as if some ghostly energy was by her side.

'Do you keep going cold? Are you cold *here*?' asked Sarah, pointing to Dianne's arms.

'Yes, I am actually,' Dianne confirmed. Then she noticed the cold area moved to her back and Sarah felt this too.

'Ghosts and spirits create a cold spot don't they?'

'Well, I'd like to think it's Dad,' Dianne replied.

'Really?' Sarah seemed excited by the idea.

Then, as if in response, the temperature immediately dropped significantly. Both women were now freezing, and with the intensity of this sensation came a really strong emotion, affecting both women in an identical manner.

'I'm not going to cry,' said Dianne, determined to hold it together.

But Sarah was already on her feet, rushing out of the room in floods of tears, crying for the stranger she'd never met. Almost as soon at it appeared, the feeling began to pull away. Then Dianne started to talk to Dad, having an inner conversation with him, and with each question she asked, the temperature fell drastically once more. Later, when Sarah had recovered a little and the temperature had returned to normal she came back into the room. Neither of them had felt anything quite like it before.

*

That same day, I was sitting at the computer in the conservatory at home when my daughter, Georgina, and her boyfriend Kyle stuck their heads around the door to say hello.

'Hello darling, what have you been up to?' I asked.

'Just hanging around . . .' Georgina shrugged.

'Go on. Tell her,' pushed Kyle.

'Tell me what?' I urged.

Georgina blushed and seemed reluctant to answer. Kyle jumped in, explaining, 'She told me Ron came to visit again last night.'

'Brilliant! What happened?' I asked, wondering what Dad had been up to this time.

Georgina hesitated, before sending Kyle away on some pretext, so she could explain her dream to me without feeling awkward. She then went on to explain how Granddad had showed her a scene from her future wedding (clearly, an embarrassing topic to discuss in front of her new partner). 'I think Granddad's trying to tell me he's always going to be there for important occasions, dead or alive, no matter what,' she told me.

I smiled, and she walked into my arms for a hug. 'It was real Mum; it was just like the other visit,' she said.

I believed her. Dad adored his grandchildren and their relationship with him was close throughout his life. And now in his afterlife too, it seemed. These dream visits were becoming bizarrely common.

A dream remembered

When I next saw Dianne at Mum's, she said, 'I forgot to tell you I had a strange dream the night *before* Dad died.'

'Do you remember it?' I asked her. 'We could add it to the book.' 'Yes,' she said, searching through her handbag. 'I copied it down from my journal for you. Here it is.'

With unspoken accord, we both moved into the snug. I perched on the edge of the seat in anticipation, as Dianne unfolded the piece of paper. 'I'd forgotten about this until recently and have only just realised it could have some bearing on Dad's passing.'

'Oh. So it was a dream *about* Dad – or was Dad *in* it?' I asked.

'Well, I remember there was a room full of people and I knew I had to talk to them *all;* I got dressed, as if waiting for something important to happen. But I didn't know what. Then, when I woke up in the morning I was surprised – I found that I *was* dressed!'

'What? You mean you *actually* had your clothes on?'

'Yes. I dreamed about getting dressed, ready for something important, and I'd physically put my clothes on!'

So the night before Dad passed it was as if Dianne was being prepared – literally – ready for the day ahead.

Gates of Heaven

Debbie also had a dream the night before he died. She dreamt about a pair of big white open gates, 'the gates of heaven?' I wondered afterwards. White doors and gates figure often in visits from the other side. I also had a similar dream that night, but after sharing it with the others I immediately forgot what the dream was about, which made me wonder if my dream had been just a *dream*.

'World on a String' – the encore

Meanwhile, Dad had been 'playing' the same tune all week. I'd heard 'I've Got the World on a String' in my head several times on waking up, and Mum too woke up with it in her head. We discovered this had even happened to both of us on the same morning.

Then, another day, Dianne was watching TV and had gone into the kitchen to make herself a drink. When she got back, the TV had switched channels. Irritated, Dianne turned it back to the original channel only to find Michael Bublé singing – yes, you guessed it . . .

The name or type of song is not relevant – it's just that this simple sign held meaning for *us* and it appeared again and again as the weeks went on.

Dad had definitely chosen his theme tune.

The Final Journey Home

Madeline: The morning of the funeral. Was this real? The hearse carrying Dad's coffin was now parked directly outside, I hadn't considered this, and kept my eyes averted. Dad's body may be in there, I told myself, but Dad the person – the soul that made him who he was, the essence of the man, his spirit – was certainly not.

Jacky: I didn't look at the coffin in the hearse either. I was going to be giving a eulogy at the funeral and had to keep myself calm. We talked about normal everyday things in the car on the way there, none of us daring to listen to the truth of the journey, knowing that if we started to think about the reality we might never recover. No one cried. There was no drama. The journey in the car was just something to be endured, to get through.

I saw my brother-in-law, Nick, across the car park and headed over to him. He looked sharp in his black suit, I noticed. He was going to do a reading too, so we decided to stay outside together right until the last minute.

As we stood huddled in the doorway, the wind whipping around us, a couple approached. I didn't recognise them. Perhaps they were here for another funeral and had come to the wrong door?

'Excuse me?' one of them asked, looking directly at Nick. 'Can you show us where the toilets are?'

'Er . . . sorry . . . ' began Nick. Then, realising the confusion, he said, 'Oh – I don't work here!'

The couple walked away embarrassed. But they'd broken our sombre mood, and Nick turned to me, grinning: 'Do I really look like a funeral director?' he asked.

And so it was that Nick and I were giggling as we were beckoned into the chapel. Someone up there *must* have set that one up! Laughter was Dad's style, and Eric's, and that amusing little scenario set the tone for the whole funeral.

Strangely, the funeral was magical. Crowds and crowds of people had gathered to honour my father. All in all we had around a hundred people in the chapel – a great turnout for a man of seventy-seven, and I remembered my dream the week before in which Dad had said, 'I can't believe how many people have come!' He was right. In Dad's heavenly timeline he had glimpsed ahead to his funeral and been pleased. He had the send-off he deserved.

I smiled as I looked around me. And people looked

grateful for my smiles. But little did they know that I was smiling at the scene from outside the chapel that was playing over and over in my mind as Nick and I now waited our turns to speak.

I was amazingly calm. It was as if someone on high was giving me the strength I needed to do my piece – a poem I'd written for the occasion. I pretended I was running a workshop, smiling again as I walked up to the podium, just as I'd done in my professional life, many times before.

Madeline: I designed the order of service, with everyone's approval: simple black text on a plain white sheet adorned on the front with just a small, ethereal dove. The dove represents, among other things, the spirit of the departed loved one being released to begin the final journey home; it is also symbolic of a being that belongs to the Earth, yet is capable of existing in the skies. But even without reading anything deeper into the image, I was happy with the way it looked on the page.

Mum was surrounded by a protective circle of sons-in-law at the chapel. I followed late and sat next to her. I tried to stay focused; I didn't want to cry all day.

Jacky read her poem, 'In Heaven'. She did such a good job that I wanted to clap when she stood down, and later other people said they felt the same, but no one stirred. Then two of Ron's sons-in-law followed with readings of their own. Everyone was brilliant.

'Top of the World' by the Carpenters played out loud and clear. The curtains stayed open around the coffin. We'd hung a bunch of three wooden fish and a small sign saying 'Gone Fishing' on the side. It was perfect. We also laid out Dad's

Masonic regalia – an elaborately embroidered piece of uniform – in recognition of his status at his lodge. Fishing and Freemasonry – after his family, these were his favourite things.

Jacky: After the service, people came up and congratulated us. 'I've never been to a funeral like that before,' they said. 'It summed up your dad beautifully', 'It was just as I'd remembered him', 'What a great funeral.'

Finally, as we got back in the car to leave, the funeral director came over to us. 'I just wanted to check something with you,' she began cautiously. 'We've just tipped out the money from the collection box and someone has added a packet of mints. I wondered if this means anything special to you?' she asked.

We all nodded and grinned as she handed the mints through the window. Dad had always had a mint in his mouth! Once again, there was that little touch of humour. And there were still more surprises to come . . .

Chapter 10

Call me when you get to heaven

Our truest life is when we are in our dreams awake.

Henry David Thoreau

The Send-off

Jacky: We invited everyone back to the bungalow to celebrate the wonderful life of this extraordinary man. We'd spent the evening before preparing refreshments for our guests; catering for all those people gave us a much-needed distraction. We'd also taped notices to the walls with arrows giving directions to toilets, food and 'bar' areas. Madeline and I got really carried away with this, and the signs covered every available space – on cupboards, behind doors and on windows; it became a bit of a joke and helped to lighten the mood. We also tacked piles of sympathy cards to the windows and walls, having long-since run out of shelf space. Many of the sympathy cards contained money, donated towards a bench in Dad's name and a local charity.

We covered three tables with food, while bottles of wine and spirits crowded the kitchen worktops. I made sure that Dad's precious bottle-opener penknife – the one he'd shown me in the dream – had pride of place in the bar area. He would have loved it!

Many people said it was the best funeral they'd ever been to; someone even commented that when the music had played in the chapel of rest they'd felt like dancing!

As often happens, there were people there that day we hadn't seen for years. I created memory sheets so that everyone could record their special thoughts about Dad. Lots of people filled them in. The grandchildren's stories were the funniest. 'Grand-dad would spend hours telling us very long "interesting" stories about fishing . . . ' one said. But the light, sarcastic humour of the teenagers didn't hide their great fondness and love.

The Last Piece of the Puzzle

The day after her granddad's funeral, Charlotte, Dad's eldest grandchild, had her driving test. We were all stunned that she was brave enough to go ahead with it, but she was determined. Afterwards, she walked through the door and waved her car keys at us – we realised she'd passed and we all rushed over to hug her. I was so proud, I burst into tears. We all needed the good news after the sad week we'd had and there soon wasn't a dry eye in the place.

Then I remembered. The wallet full of cash . . . the penknife bottle-opener . . . and, of course, the car key. Dad had showed me a car key in the dream. The last part of the puzzle was now in place. Dad had been aware of Charlotte's success in her driving test days before she'd even taken it!

' . . . World on a String' – Again

Madeline: We stayed as late as possible on our last day at Mum's, finally leaving about 7.30 p.m. Although we knew we'd be back in five weeks' time to help Mum move house, it was tough leaving her. But we usually spent a great deal of time talking on the telephone, and I knew things would be no different now.

Just a week later, young Jim, a big music fan, asked if he could borrow some money to buy a CD in the local super-market. On the same display as the CD he wanted we spotted a Frank Sinatra box set at a really good price. There were four CDs in the set and the first song on the first side was 'I've Got the World on a String'. There it was again – and we just had to buy it!

Georgina Sees Granddad . . .

Jacky: Nearly two weeks after the funeral, Georgina had another visit from her Granddad. 'I was lying asleep in bed, and I dreamed that I was a passenger in Kyle's car,' she told me. 'Then I called your mobile to see where you all were. You told me you were at a restaurant. So Kyle and I drove over to try and find you.'

'Then what happened?' I asked, intrigued.

'When we walked into the restaurant I saw a man that looked just like Granddad. He was sitting on a sofa next to Aunty Madeline. I thought it *was* Granddad, but then I realised it couldn't be Granddad, because Granddad was dead.'

'So you were awake during the dream then, if you realised he'd died?'

'Yes, I absolutely knew what was going on, Mum. The rest of the women in the family were there too. I wondered if you were with this man because he reminded you of Granddad. He was tanned and smiling. Then I got closer and he asked me for a hug and I realised it actually *was* Granddad! I was really surprised because in the dream he was alive.'

'How wonderful!'

'As he hugged me, I was standing and he stayed sitting down. I asked him how he'd been able to be with the family since he'd died, and he explained that after he died he just woke up again.'

Georgina said she asked her Granddad to explain what happened when he passed, and he told her that it felt like a bang in his chest and then he didn't see anything. The next thing he knew it was about a week later (in his new time); he said he woke up and realised he was OK – dead, but OK.

The dream scene then changed and Georgina found herself in a boat on a fishing lake. Granddad was rowing.

'I told Granddad, "I trust you",' she said, 'because I was facing backwards.'

'Were you wary because of your car accident?' I asked.

'Yes.'

Georgina had been involved in an accident months earlier. She was a passenger in a car which had rolled over and over, landing in a ditch that was full of water, following extensive rain. The vehicle had landed upside down under the water, and Georgina had feared she might drown.

'Granddad told me he was fine and wanted to know why I'd been crying. I told him I couldn't understand what was happening because we'd been to his funeral and everything. How could he be talking to me now? It was then that he reassured me, he was "OK", and he really *was* "alive", so I should stop worrying.'

Granddad then rowed Georgina to the side of the bank where her nan was waiting. Her nan told her, 'We must contact everyone to let them know that Granddad is OK.' Then Georgina woke up.

As I typed up Georgina's 'visit', I began to explore some of the subtle messages that were hidden inside.

I considered that the boat might be symbolic of the mode of travel from one realm to the next. The lake (Dad's 'realm') could be reached for short visits, so that Dad can visit us and we can visit him. He could 'row' out to get us, (thereby using his energy, in dreams and so on) or maybe we could 'row' ourselves, in our own boat, meeting him in *his* space (through deep meditation techniques, for example).

In the dream visit Mum had said, 'We must contact everyone to let them know that Granddad is OK.' Dad seemed to be giving us permission to tell his story, using Mum to pass on his message – permission from them both, on a soul level, perhaps? There seems to be a universal law of 'free will', whereby we make our own choices – and mistakes – in life. But Dad was giving us his blessing, without telling us what to do. It made perfect sense.

Although I'd given Georgina copies of all my books, she had never read any of them as she didn't want my work to influence her own life experiences. So she knew that what she was going through now was happening spontaneously and without any manipulation from others – least of all her mum!

... and Kyle sees 'Granddad' too

It was now over three weeks since the funeral. Georgina was lying in the bath, when Kyle rang her on her mobile and began to recount an experience from the night before.

'I remember walking up the stairs to the spare bedroom at my grandmother's house. I sat down on the bed, put the TV on and the next thing I knew, it was morning. I was still dressed. I've never fallen asleep so quickly in all my life. Oh, and I had a *weird* dream.'

'What about?'

'Well, I dreamed that I was sitting in the living room at my grandmother's. I looked up and Ron walked into the room.

'What – Granddad?'

'Yes, your granddad! He was laughing and smiling, and he came and sat down next to me. We were watching a black and white movie; it was a western. We were sort of "hanging out" together and having fun.'

'Granddad loved old movies.' Georgina smiled.

Kyle went on to say that the scene then cut, and he found himself sitting with Dad on the bank of a horseshoe lake. He described this to Georgina: 'The sun was setting and the colours in the sky were the most beautiful I'd ever seen. Everything was so vivid. Ron was fishing and caught a large fish, and was very excited about it. I was in awe and said, although I'd been fishing several times in my life I'd never caught *anything*. Ron turned to me and said, 'Your time will come." Then he stood up, but before he walked away he turned back to face me and said, 'Take good care of her.' And I knew he meant for me to look after *you*, Georgina.'

'You know, that sounds like one of those "visits" that Mum talks about,' Georgina said. By now, she had started to recognise a few of the signs. Boyfriend Kyle had been instrumental in bringing through a message for the family as well as for himself, and this was the first visitation experience from someone *outside* the family. Knowing nothing of psychic phenomena he only shared it with his girlfriend because it had been such a powerful and unusual dream. But Georgina later encouraged a reluctant Kyle to share his dream with me. And I realised immediately that this was no ordinary dream.

The way that Kyle fell into such a sudden and deep sleep that night may or may not be relevant, but Dad walking through the door is a classic symbol of afterlife visitation. Other signs include walking through a gate, appearing through a tunnel, or walking out of a light. These signs all act as ways of indicating that the spirit has come from 'another place' or another realm.

A shared love of black and white movies was a great way to make Kyle feel comfortable at the beginning of the visitation. I'm sure Dad was cautious about his approach to the young teenager he barely knew.

Beautiful colours, such as Kyle mentioned, are often seen by people during a near-death experience too. Colours not known or recognised on Earth can sometimes be seen during spirit visitation. Kyle was unsure if he'd seen *new* colours, when I asked him, but recalled it being unlike *anything* he'd ever experienced in his life; it was 'breathtaking', he told me.

It's very likely that the message 'Your time will come' referred to much more than catching a fish. Dad seemed almost to be checking Kyle out – to see if he made suitable boyfriend material. And we all felt he'd probably passed the test! Maybe the 'big fish' in Kyle's future is a 'catch' of another sort?

Also, Dad was once again using a lake in the vision – again, to reference his realm, perhaps. This time Dad has made his way to Kyle's 'space' by sitting with him at the edge of the lake. Kyle had only met Dad on two or three occasions before he died, so the dream visitation is particularly significant as a piece of afterlife evidence.

Although reluctant to share his experience at first, and slightly embarrassed too, Kyle was *very* comfortable on discovering that his vivid 'dream' may well have been something more!

I was reminded of my earliest visit, two nights after Dad died, in which he and Eric were on a beach drinking cocktails. Although I'd been sitting on the beach with them, I was only an observer as they'd jumped into the speedboats and dived into the water. Perhaps I too had been right on the edge of their realm?

Fit and Healthy on the Other-Side

I rang Debbie early the following day to tell her about Kyle's dream, but before I had the opportunity to explain, Debbie told me that *she'd* had another visit the night before.

'I saw Dad again last night,' she began. 'He was skipping through some spring flowers. There were loads of them – daffodils, tulips and crocuses. It's like he was showing me how fit he was and said, "Look what I can do now!" Then he looked at me with concern and said, "Stop crying. I'm right here!"'

'Are you still crying?' I asked.

'Yes – well I cried last night.'

'Well, we *are* going to cry for a long time; it's still so raw.'

'But it's like he knows what's going on in our lives – like he'd seen me crying.'

'He would have felt the emotion. Our emotions are what bring them to us. It's the love that connects us,' I explained.

'Dad was surrounded by relatives – all dead ones!' she continued. 'I could see his mum and dad, his Uncle Bert and Aunty Nell, our grandparents and Mum's brother Billy. And there were stacks of dogs with him; dogs from our family – Susie and Candy. He told me, "Candy doesn't bite any more." And he had a collie too.'

'Remember that collie-cross that John and I had when the kids were small? And didn't Eric keep collies as well?'

'Oh – yes. And there was another dog called Suki that I didn't know,' Debbie added.

'What did that one look like?'

'Small, black and rough-haired ... Jacky, Dad looked so well. Really young and fit; but then suddenly he looked older again, like he wanted to make sure I recognised him! Oh, and there were other people I didn't recognise as well. He wanted me to know I had no reason to be sad; he was happy, fit and most importantly, was not alone.'

Debbie was already beginning to analyse her own dream, and was spot on as to why Dad had shown himself as young, healthy and in good company.

Although I'd told Debbie that Dad could *feel* our emotions, I felt he could also *see* what was happening; he'd asked Georgina why *she* was crying, and had gone on to reassure them both that he was OK.

As for the dogs, Debbie emailed Madeline about the pets in her dream, and Madeline remembered a photo *she* had at home. In the picture Dad is a young man and he's stroking a small, black, rough-haired dog – exactly the sort of dog that Debbie described. Sadly, there was no one alive who could confirm the dog's name.

I've since discovered that deceased pets are common to spirit visitations. And spirits – including pets – will commonly appear younger than the age at which they passed, showing themselves as they looked at their best – or better! So people with disabilities or missing limbs will nearly always be whole when they visit as spirits – unless they use the disability to help you to recognise them. Dad was not only without his walking stick in Debbie's dream, he was skipping! Now I don't know that I'd *ever* seen him do that; but there were plenty more 'firsts' from Dad in the pipeline!

Chapter 11

From old dogs to new tricks

An idea, like a ghost, must be spoken to a little
before it will explain itself.

Charles Dickens

Record Keepers

Madeline: The more Dad communicated with us, the more
we began to understand and unravel the messages he was
bringing: some were funny, like the perfectly timed door
chimes, which always made us laugh; some were moving, like
the dreams with hugs and dancing; some were predictive, as
he gave us information about what would happen in the
future; and some were spiritually profound, as he gave us
insights into his death and the afterlife.

The messages and visits continued, and we kept careful
records of all unusual happenings. Again, individual occur-
rences are easy to pass over, overlook or ignore. But by
gathering the phenomena together, and looking at them

collectively, we realised what a fantastic compilation we had amassed. As recently bereaved family and friends who were open to the 'possibilities', we felt privileged to be in a position of being able to bring all this afterlife evidence together in this way and publish the results.

Unmistakable – Dad Calling

Jacky: Mum had a visit one day from some very dear friends. The couple were in Egypt when Dad died and were devastated to have missed their old friend's funeral.

The three of them were sitting in the dining room, Mum sharing details of Dad's final days, when the inevitable single-ring doorbell chimed. When Mum didn't get up to answer the door, her friends looked confused. Mum then explained that the single ring meant that Dad was 'calling', and acknowledging their visit, as he'd done with other special contacts in the last few weeks. She went to the door to reassure them. And, as usual, no one was there. The doorbell *never* rang its single 'spirit' ring after dark, and it was never scary. Dad seemed simply to be taking the opportunity to acknowledge all of his friends, one at a time, by ringing the doorbell or blinking the lights, saying a final farewell.

'Music for Cool Dads'

John and I decided to spend a day out together over the Easter weekend. It was time for a break. A belief in the afterlife helps the grieving process a lot, but I still ached all over from stress.

We went to a country home owned by the National Trust called Hardwick Hall. In the gift shop there, I walked over to a display of CDs and picked up one that was called 'Music for Cool Dads'. The cover was designed in an old-fashioned style with a drawing of two men, dressed in 1950s-style cardigans. Although it was not the sort of CD I'd usually be drawn to, I started casually to read the back cover and laughed out loud when I saw 'I've Got the World on a String' on the list of tracks. I immediately rushed out to tell John as it seemed such a strange coincidence. Although maybe it was time to stop using the word 'coincidence'?

Dad Puts the Kettle On

The following day, John and I went to visit Mum. Sisters Debbie and Dianne were both there when we arrived, sorting through kitchen cupboards in preparation for the move.

We sat with Mum in the snug, talking to her about our wedding anniversary arrangements, although this was not until the following February. Mum was concerned about our elaborate plans and what they might cost. She suggested that the money might be better spent on a deposit for a new house.

I disagreed and told Mum that I felt my family were more important than a house. And just as I expressed this sentiment, the kettle clicked on in the kitchen (it sounded so loud, even from the other room) and, at the same time, we could hear Debbie and Dianne laughing in the kitchen. 'Dad agrees,' they called out. And we realised that the kettle had switched *itself* on.

Dianne told me later that the two of them had, at first, tried to explain away the incident. Had they knocked into the kettle?

Perhaps they'd slammed a cupboard door? Or maybe the kettle was faulty? It had never switched on by itself before – or since, for that matter. No – this was clearly another 'unexplainable' phenomenon during the weeks after Dad's passing. Another perfectly timed moment, in my opinion.

Comfort From the Other Side

Nearly four weeks after Dad had passed, Debbie and I were chatting about how people grieve for the loss of physical touch from a deceased loved one. We talked about how both my daughter, Georgina, and our sister, Madeline, had experienced physical touch in their dream visitations from Dad. Georgina had felt a very real hug and Madeline had danced with Dad. It seemed that 'touch' can still happen from the other side of life too.

So when Debbie phoned me the following morning, I wondered if Dad might have been listening in on our conversation.

'I was asleep in bed when Dad came and hugged me,' she told me. 'Nothing else happened, but he hugged me for a long time. I know it was him, as I'd been crying again and was upset that he'd died. No one else was in the room, but I knew it was real.'

'It's strange isn't it?' I said, before asking, 'Did you see him?'

'No, I only felt him. When you've known someone for over forty years, and been comforted by those loving arms, you don't forget that feeling in a hurry, do you?'

Amazingly, hugs and real touches – where the 'dream' sensation feels extraordinarily lifelike – can really be an occasional part of a dream visitation experience. Usually, the touch part of the dream visit is short or the spirit becomes invisible for the duration of the physical contact.

In my research, I've investigated many cases of afterlife contact where spirits themselves have explained that it is hard for them to be seen *and* touched at the same time. I realised that for a spirit to maintain physical contact for as long as Dad had when he'd held Madeline for a ballroom dance was very rare. I'm sure Dad was given a lot of help from the other side to manifest this phenomenon.

Dad at the Wheel

One of the things Dad had missed most in his final year was driving. He'd driven a car for all of his adult life and, in the months before his passing, he hadn't been well enough to do so – a bitter blow to both his self-esteem and his lifestyle. I wasn't surprised, therefore, when Dianne shared her next dream visit with me.

'I was sitting in Dad's car and he was driving,' she told me.

'I guess if you can do *anything* in heaven, he was bound to turn up in a car at some point,' I laughed.

'Exactly! He was driving and we were having a good chat, although I don't recall what we talked about. We were visiting some of the places I remembered as a child, even our old house.'

'I've heard about spirits appearing in cars before and, in some cases, planes and motorbikes; do you remember I saw Dad and Eric in speedboats in my dream?'

'Oh yes, that's right. Anyway, when we arrived at the old house it looked just the way it used to. I don't remember getting out of the car, but we must have done because we looked around the whole house. The stair rail was the one thing that really stood out. When I touched the banister, it felt like a solid piece of wood.'

'What? You could actually *feel* the wood in your dream?' I asked, intrigued.

'Yes,' Dianne confirmed. 'That's how I knew it wasn't an ordinary dream.'

'Fascinating – tell me more . . .'

'When we went into Mum and Dad's bedroom I wondered why there wasn't a vanity sink in the room, but I realised later that there hadn't been one, anyway – not at *that* house. The furniture was the same as it had been when Mum and Dad lived there; the garage and everything. And guess what? Our grandmother was in her room, and Dad and I chatted to her too!'

Our grandmother who'd lived with our parents, had been deceased for many years. Dianne continued, 'Then Dad drove us to Pat and Terry's house.' Mum and Dad's friend, Pat, had died some years earlier too. Dianne explained:

'It was Pat who was talking to Dad. Terry didn't speak during the whole visit, and just sat in the chair. Pat was standing; she was smoking a cigarette.'

'Oh – I'd forgotten Pat smoked,' I said. 'Terry's very ill, isn't he; maybe that's why he didn't speak in the dream – his spirit is only partly on the other side?'

'Yes, I know,' Dianne agreed. 'Mum hasn't heard from him in a while.'

I thought it interesting that Dianne had been able to touch the banister rail. And fascinating that Dad shared this visitation with our late grandmother, and his deceased friend Pat. Quite a reunion! With each visit, Dad was giving us more insight about what was possible when visiting from the afterlife.

Funny Granddad

By now, Debbie's daughter Jasmine had heard about some of our experiences and made it clear that she *didn't* want a visit from her granddad, as she was convinced she'd be way too scared. But after being reassured by her family that all the visitation experiences had been both positive and loving she had the following dream. It is difficult to decide if this experience is a visitation or not. If it is, then it would be clear that the experience was meant to amuse her; there is certainly nothing scary about it. Jasmine told me:

'In my dream Nanny was sitting in a wheelchair – the one we used for Granddad when he was poorly. It was funny because Granddad was sitting on Nanny's lap, as if he was coming along for the ride! Then we all got into the car and Nanny sat in the front seat. I could see that Granddad was sitting on her lap again, which was funny because he would never have been able to do that in life.'

This dream does seem weird, although an explanation might help. During several of Dad's illnesses the family had borrowed a wheelchair, and we'd pushed him around in it so that he wouldn't miss out on any family outings. Mum has never needed a wheelchair, of course, but I wondered if Dad might be showing that he is aware that *she* is now getting the attention which was bestowed upon *him* when alive. Or perhaps Dad was showing how he does still come along for the ride?

After Jasmine's dream, all seemed to go quiet for a couple of days. I'd been pondering this and was feeling sad that not only had I not heard any more, but no one else had reported in either. But three days after Jasmine's dream I had another sign.

More Tea?

I'd been watching the Living TV show, *Most Haunted Live*. I once appeared as a guest on the programme and still liked to tune in from time to time to see any old friends of mine who regularly appear on the show. During the break, I decided to make a hot drink before going to bed. Watching the ghost-hunting show I was already on 'high alert', so to speak.

I switched on the kettle and, as it boiled, the lid popped up all on its own! This only happens when you press a button at the side and I hadn't touched the kettle or been anywhere near it at the time. I laughed as I remembered the strange phenomenon of the kettle switching itself on at Mum's a few days earlier. Could messing with kettles be Dad's new game, I wondered.

I guess there could have been a logical explanation, but I couldn't think of one, so I simply said, 'Good night Dad'.

Doorbell – on Cue Again

One day, when Dianne was at Mum's sorting out her bank details, she was sitting at the computer, when Dad came to call.

'No sooner had I typed in Dad's name than the doorbell rang,' she told me. 'Dave [her husband] was in the garage and came in to the house to see who was at the door. There was nobody there! [Notice we still kept checking though!] As soon as Dave realised that no one was there, he scurried back into the garage, bemused!'

Life Carries On

I'd always imagined that when Dad finally died I would take to my bed in grief. The shock of losing such a special and loving man in my life would, I was sure, drive me to hide myself away. Yet life carried on much as before.

With Mum's moving date imminent, the bungalow no longer looked like Mum and Dad's home as, bit by bit, pieces of furniture were sold and taken away. We all seemed to come back from visits to the bungalow with arms full of stuff that no one could bear to throw away: perfectly good dish cloths, old plastic jugs and trays which no one liked the pattern on. We were simply moving unwanted objects from one house to the next!

Debbie, Dianne and I also spent a lot of quality time with Mum. The four of us went to the cinema together, we went shopping, visited garden centres and attended make-up parties, all the while spending lots of money. It was as if we wanted to build some new memories together – all of us frightened and all wanting to show that we could still live full and active lives for Dad's sake.

We relished the fact that Mum had begun spending money on herself for the first time ever. It was delightful to see her pick up beautiful accessories for her new apartment. Cream carpets, gold tassels and all manner of gorgeous finishes were chosen. She was enjoying the prospect of the move; we all were. Each visitor to the house was despatched around the corner to view the new apartment building, and each, in turn, was comforted that Mum too was literally going to 'a better place'.

Days would pass with no tears, but night-time was always the hardest for us all. In bed, at the end of the day, I would feel Dad's connection. It always made me shed a few tears before I got myself back together. At no point had I felt like 'letting it all out' though. That normal grieving process seemed to have completely passed me by.

Health Caution From Dad

It was now a full month since the funeral, and I had another dream. Dad was telling me something important about Mum's health. I saw Mum in hospital being examined by doctors. Dad was reassuring me in the dream.

'Even if the doctors say there is something seriously wrong with her, you mustn't worry as she's going to be fine,' he explained.

I must have looked confused, as he then said, 'She's very strong. She's got many, many birthdays yet.' Then he indicated an age close to Mum's own mother, who'd lived well into her nineties.

I shared the dream with Mum the following day and we actually laughed about it. She told me she was fine and that there wasn't anything wrong with her. Mum was *never* ill. It had always been about Dad.

'Perhaps he was telling me about something which is coming up in the future?' I suggested. 'Maybe he knows we've been through so much and doesn't want us to worry?'

Again, we laughed it off, although I still retained a niggling doubt. All the dream visits I'd had to date had been *so* real and this one was no different. But we had enough going on for now, so I 'filed' the dream away to the back of my mind where it remained . . . for just a little while longer.

Chapter 12

Is anybody there?

... I looked and saw a door opened in heaven, and
the first voice that I heard ... was one saying, 'Come
up here, and I will show you the things which must
happen after this.'

The Bible, Revelation 4:1

An Introduction to a Séance

Jacky and Madeline: Dianne and her friend, Janice, went to
visit a local medium called Pauline, who used an Ouija board.
Pauline was not only an expert and well-respected spirit com-
municator, she was also a lovely, down-to-earth lady whose
personality shone through in her work.

Dianne told us, 'Pauline felt that Dad walked in the door with
me, and even before we started the session she was picking up
information from him: "Someone is wearing his watch ... it's
gold in colour," she told me, but I said I didn't know about this.
Then she continued, "He's pleased they're wearing it."'

Jacky: As I mentioned earlier, just before Dad died, I took his watch to the hospital. He never wore it again, but I kept it on my wrist for several days after he passed. Then Mum offered the watch to my husband John, who has worn it ever since. And yes – it is gold in colour!

What follows is the fascinating transcript of Dianne's session with Pauline. We have only taken out one or two very personal details, which we later discovered were very accurate indeed.

Pauline: Any spirit friend who wishes to communicate, come to me please. *To the spirit*: Blooming heck ... you're in a hurry, my darling – go back to the centre, my ducky. If there is a spirit friend in this room, please go to the person you wish to communicate with. *The glass moves towards Dianne; the medium picks something up in her head and says out loud*: So you're her dad?

Dianne: *Dianne nods to the question directed at Ron*: Yeah.

Pauline: He brought you up good, he's saying. *To the spirit*: Right, if you're her dad, show us some proof. *To Dianne*: Ask him for his Christian name; spell out your Christian name.

Dianne: Dad, please spell out your name.

Pauline: What's your Christian name, darling – give us your Christian name. Oh all right, he's just said, 'I'm not far away from you', you understand? *To the spirit*: We know that, ducky, but what's your name? What're you doing, ducky? Come on, what's your name? *The medium is trying to encourage the spirit to use the Ouija board to spell out his name. Eventually, the glass begins to move around the letters on the board*. He's looking at the letters. Has he gone by it? Come on what's your name? Was he good at spelling?

Dianne: Yeah. *Dianne is strangely quiet, giving nothing away.*

Pauline: *To the spirit*: Come on, darling – until you've spelled your name we can't start! *With everyone's fingers on the glass it moves to the letter R.* It begins with that does it?

Dianne: Yeah, R.

Pauline: It's Ron, isn't it? He said Ronald to me ages ago. *The medium seems to have picked this information up directly from the spirit, indicating that it is, in fact, Dad; spells out RON on the board, then she asks Janice if she knew him. To Janice:* He keeps looking at you. He's just saying, 'Oh, it's lovely to see you.' *Dad was always polite and had met Janice, but wasn't well acquainted with her.*

Dianne: Ask him to spell out Dad's wife's name.

Pauline: *Spells out MARGARET.* Did he call her Marg – no, Maggie? *There was no confirmation from Dianne here, but Mum was always known as Maggie. To the spirit*: Where did you live? As we don't want any Tom, Dick or Harry coming in, do we my love. Spell it.

Dianne: Yeah. *WESTMEAD is spelled out; at the time of Dad's death, he and Mum lived in a place called Westmead Road.*

Pauline: He said is everybody coping all right?

Dianne: Yeah. I think so.

Pauline: *Passing a message from Dad*: I hope so. *Then to Dad*: What sort of work did you do? *And to Dianne*: Did he work before he died?

Dianne: No. Retired.

Pauline: Where did you work, Ron? *To Dianne*: Has he started it?

Dianne: Yeah.

Pauline: Come on, Ron. Finish it. *To Dianne*: Is he doing it?

Dianne: Yeah. Started again. *INCA is spelled out.*

Pauline: Inca. What's Inca?

Dianne: It's jewellery. *Inca was the name of the company Dad had sold jewellery for for many years.*

Pauline: What's to do with the brewery, then? *Dad appears to be communicating directly with the medium here.*

Dianne: I work for the brewery.

Pauline: But it's not Ind Coope you work for, is it?

Dianne: No. Dad was unlikely to remember the name.

Pauline: Oh – an example. Ask him anything.

Dianne: Gone blank. Don't know what to ask. Dad, will Mum be OK and will you be keeping and eye on her?

Pauline: She needs you all; has she been looking at photos? Is there a big one?

Dianne: Yes, it's of Mum and Dad. It's on her phone now. *Mum had a large photograph of her and Dad which we reframed. Someone took a photograph of it on her mobile phone, so she can carry it around with her. And she had been sorting out the photos over the previous few days.*

Pauline: He knows all about it.

Dianne: Will Mum still be moving house? *Although Mum was planning a move to the local apartment we'd found, there'd been a few problems which slowed things down.*

Pauline: When she is ready.

Dianne: Ask where she's moving to.

Pauline: *Hears a message in her head from Dad and tells Dianne*: She'll be on one level . . . saying there is a lift.

Dianne: *Laughing*: Yes, he knows about the lift. *Thinking*: Oh yes, bless – he knows about the lift as he got caught by the lift door one day, bless him.

MEWS is then spelled out; the name of the new apartment contains the word Mews.

Pauline: You'll be right soon; just go with the changes. You understand? *Then, about Dianne's husband*: What's her husband's name? Is he doing it?

Dianne: *DAVID is spelled out in full.* Yeah!

Pauline: Sometimes called him DAVID. *He was also called Dave.* He liked him. *They were great friends.* What did you and her husband do together? *Spells out FISH, which is correct.* Did you go somewhere special? Where was it? Where did you go fishing Ron? *Spells out MAKIN, which is, again, correct.* Where's that then?

Dianne: Out Hinckley way. *Glass zooms to the word* YES.

Pauline: Where has Dianne moved to now? Where does she live now? What road does she live on? *Spells out WOODBINE, which is correct; Dad had visited the house many times. The glass starts to move again and spells out a well-known name.*

Dianne: Hold on. *Laughing*: I know what he's spelling. *Spells ERIC.*

Janice: He's spelling ERIC!

Pauline: Spelling Eric? Who's Eric?

Dianne: He's my Dad's brother and ... we always talk about Uncle Eric.

Pauline: Right. Is Eric dead then?

Dianne: Yes ... Dad's started to ring the doorbell. *Dianne explains the doorbell-ringing incidents and Dad replies through the medium.*

Pauline: He said, 'Good, innit?' Ask what you want to know.

Dianne: I don't know what I want to know. *There is slight panic in her voice at the possibility she might miss the opportunity of asking questions.*

Pauline: What's that dog you've got? What's the dog's name, Ron? Come on, darling. *Spells CANDY, our childhood pet.* What's the other one called — Candy and who? *She asks the question, but then gets the answer.* It was a girl dog. Was it Susie or something?

Dianne: Yeah.

Pauline: Ask any question.

Dianne: Will Dad work with me?

Pauline: He's only a thought away.

Dianne: . . . I'm picking him up a lot around me.

Pauline: It's not your imagination. He wouldn't let you down . . . ticking noise in car? It's Dad. He looks after you and your car. Are you thinking of changing the car?

Dianne: Yes.

Pauline: Is it running well? Why change it? *Pauline looks at Dianne.* Did you know you were a pleasure — heh? You could communicate with him.

Dianne: I wanted to treasure the time I had with him. *Spells LOVE YOU ALWAYS.* Do you remember the last thing I called you — although it wasn't me, it was Debbie that told you?

Pauline: What did she call you?

Dianne: . . . started it . . . I'm getting upset . . .

Pauline: He's upset as well now.

Dianne: Keeps starting to spell it. *Spells MOTHER TERESA. Dianne explains they'd called him Mother Teresa after wrapping his head in a blue towel on his last day in hospital.*

Pauline: *Dad immediately gives the medium another name that he is called, but Dianne misses the 'clue':* Charles? Who's that? Or Charlie?

Dianne: Dad's friend.

Pauline: Have you seen him? Were you talking about Dad?

Dianne: Yes. At Dad's funeral.

[*Note from Madeline: Actually, when I read through this transcript, the first thing that occurred to me was that Dad's son-in-law always called him 'Charles', usually in a funny voice – 'Ahh, Charles, how the devil are you?' Or he would call him 'Ice-tart Charlie' because they both loved Iced Tarts – the cakes! They could be quite greedy with them, and it was a bit of a standing joke in the family. Dad's friend Charles was never called Charlie, so I feel sure this is a reference to Dad's own nickname – it was even mentioned in the reading at his funeral. Both Dianne and then Jacky, when she transcribed the session, missed this; we feel this is what a medium would call great 'evidence' of the afterlife. Once I had pointed it out to them they both agreed that this was definitely the 'Charlie' he was talking about.*]

Pauline: *A vague and general question at first*: Was your dad ever connected with a uniform or anything?

Dianne: Yes, he was.

Pauline: He's standing tall, like he would be proud.

[*Funny – we used the words proud and tall in his obituary; it describes Dad exactly.*]

Dianne: Dad – will you spell out the uniform thing you wore?

Pauline: Is he doing it? Was it green? He's standing like he's proud. Dad's National Service uniform was green. *Spells MASONIC*. Where was it Ron? Where are the Masons?

Dianne: Dad, spell the name of the house. *Meaning the Masonic meeting hall.*

Pauline: Ron, spell the name of the house. *Spells ASH-FIELD HOUSE, which is correct.* Ron says he must go now, but he's not far away. Sends his love to all.

For the family, this was an amazing session. Many times, the answers appeared to come directly through the medium and were not even being spelled out. The medium did not have access to this personal information about our father (some of it obscure – like the dog's name), so if she wasn't *channelling* the thoughts from the 'other side', she must have been great at mind-reading (admittedly, a brilliant skill in itself). Of course, even Dianne didn't remember the 'Charlie' reference, so that was particularly intriguing.

If there *is* another explanation to this exceptional piece of mediumship, we don't have it. It truly was a first-rate illustration of astounding contact from the 'other side'. What on earth was going to happen next?

Chapter 13

Life — but not as we know it

> Reality is merely an illusion, albeit a very
> persistent one.
>
> *Albert Einstein*

Father-in-Law Visits

Jacky: It was 10 April, and around six weeks since Dad's passing. I was chatting to Mum about how Dad had 'gone quiet' again and I said how much I was missing him and wished he would visit. We also talked about some of the other dream visits I'd had over the years, especially those from Dad's brother Eric and my father-in-law Jack.

That night, I went to sleep as normal, and then woke in the morning to say goodbye to John before falling back to sleep again. It was during this later snooze that I had a dream visitation from Jack.

In the dream, I was sitting in the living room of a previous house, when he walked in. He looked so well, and younger and slimmer than when he was alive. It was wonderful to see him. He sat on the sofa and I sat on the chair; I was explaining to him about the different types of psychic phenomena that the family had experienced since Dad died. He seemed really interested, and I was excited to share this with him.

While we were talking, an old record player in the room started spinning round on its own and the two of us laughed. I was still in mid-conversation in my dream, when the telephone rang beside my bed and woke me up. I felt cross because I knew this was a *real* visit and I wanted to carry on chatting to my father-in-law for longer.

It was John on the telephone; and it was *his* father that I'd been speaking to in my dream. John had called from work because he'd felt a 'sudden urge' to ring me. It wasn't even important; he just wanted me to telephone some friends to invite them for dinner. I realised he'd been 'prompted' to ring me.

Often these dream visits take place in the early hours of the morning and then something wakes us up right after, so that we remember the experience. I was so surprised when John rang me that I didn't even tell him his dad had been visiting me in a dream.

I no longer felt cross that the dream had been cut short because I realised that my father-in-law Jack had stayed as long as he was able to. It was wonderful to know that the thoughts I'd shared with Mum the day before had been heard and it was lovely to know that he was still able to visit me too.

Granddad Sitting in His Arm Chair

The next day, seventeen-year-old Jasmine had another visit from Granddad, and rang her cousin, to tell her about it.

Realising there might be more to this, Charlotte excitedly handed me the phone so that I could give my diagnosis! Jasmine told me:

'In the dream, we were all at Nan's house having a big party. Nan was moving the next day and all the family were there. Then the doorbell rang and one of the boys went to answer it. I immediately heard Granddad's voice and got very excited. No one else heard him though and I felt frustrated when five other people came in the door to join the party and Granddad wasn't among them.'

'Do you know who the other people were?' I asked. 'Perhaps they were the new owners?'

'I don't know; I've never seen them before. But when I walked back into the big lounge, Granddad was sitting in his favourite chair. He had a big grin on his face and I was so excited to see him that I started jumping up and down. I was so happy and immediately went to sit on his lap just like I used to!'

'How lovely. You *know* this is real, don't you?'

'Well, I thought it might be because I did realise he was dead – that's why I was so excited to see him.'

'That's how I know it's a visitation. Because in a visitation, you *always* know the visitor is dead,' I explained.

'Yes, but I was upset that no one else had seen him. Then I went and fetched the rest of the family from the small room and then they could all see Granddad too.'

'How did he look?'

'Well, he didn't have his walking stick, but looked much as he'd done before he died. He was wearing a purple anorak with cream on the inside.'

'Then you woke up?'

'Well, my bed broke – and *then* I woke up!'

Jasmine's new bed had literally broken. This was the

strangest awakening 'trick' I've ever come across. The waking-up moment is crucial as it enables the person to remember their dream. I myself am usually woken by the telephone ringing, or sometimes by the voice of a 'living' loved one calling my name – another 'trick' because often these people aren't even in the house at the time.

Our deceased loved ones' visits are often brief; they have to pack a lot of information into a short space of time, so they sometimes use signs and symbolism to help get their messages across. The 'purple anorak' is certainly a strange one, and I don't understand if there was a message here or not. It's more usual for a spirit to wear a favourite item of clothing or something very familiar to the family. To this day, we haven't worked out why Dad wore this previously unknown garment.

The rest of the dream, however, follows classic dream visitation experiences; Jasmine knew her granddad was dead and was excited to see him, understanding that during the experience he was visiting from another dimension. And, as we've said, spirits don't need walking sticks when they're dead, but do occasionally bring such props, or glasses, for example, so that they can be easily recognised.

Positive Feelings About Death

Life had begun to take on a new sense of normality. Mum commented that she was going to accept 'every single invitation' that came her way. She was never in the house! And phone calls round the family meant we were always planning something or other. It was almost like we were catching up for lost time – time when Mum couldn't join us on 'girlie outings' because she was looking after Dad.

Rather than feeling grief, I now realised how easy it had become to imagine Dad on holiday somewhere, as I'd suggested that Charlotte should do. And with Dad 'calling home' and letting us know he was OK, this was made all the easier. Why couldn't everyone experience death in this way, I wondered. Was it that our awareness of afterlife contact meant we'd created a network to share experiences? Or maybe it was because Dad knew we would write it all down, so that others could share these experiences too. After all, he had promised to help us write a book.

I'd certainly heard and written about hundreds of stories of afterlife contact. Many people were receiving contact in this way – people would write to me through my website and share a 'weird' dream or a 'bizarre' experience relating to the loss of a loved one. But Dad *was* definitely visiting us more than was 'usual', and I loved that so many independent people were experiencing visitations from him too. It really helped to build a picture of afterlife contact.

On the 13 April 2008 it was my youngest daughter Georgina's seventeenth birthday. Another family celebration without Granddad ... without Dad.

Old Tricks ... and New

Debbie took her friend, Sue, round to Mum's bungalow, as she was interested in buying Mum's old TV. With just a few days left before moving day, we were tying to clear out as much stuff as possible. Mum was out to lunch, but Debbie held a spare key. And while they were there, they had a visit from Dad.

Debbie told me, 'I showed Sue the montage of Dad's photographs that Georgina had created for the funeral.' This was a large board with a selection of our favourite photographs of Dad, many of him laughing and smiling. She went on, 'Sue was admiring the photographs, in particular, photos of Dad with us. Right on cue, the doorbell rang, and when I didn't immediately rush to answer it, Sue asked me why. I told her it was Dad at the door and she looked perplexed. I took her hand and led her to the front door. No one was there . . . apart from Dad, of course! I got Sue to ring the doorbell herself and she laughed, immediately noticing the difference between the two chimes.'

Madeline: Moving day arrived and all four of Mum's sons-in-law had taken the day off work to help, along with all four daughters and two of the adult grandchildren.

The doorbell was taken down from the front door and the speaker unplugged. But Dad was not going to be that easily deterred from communicating with us . . .

I was packing in the lounge when I heard a 'pip' noise. I rushed into the breakfast room and asked Debbie, 'Did you hear a noise?'

'What kind of a noise?' she asked.

'I'm sure I heard a single beep, like the smoke alarm or something. Did anybody else hear that?' I asked, peering around the corner into the snug. Everybody shook their heads, so I carried on wrapping the last odds and ends with my pile of newspapers.

A few minutes later, the alarm sounded again. This time all the others heard it, and we acknowledged Dad as the culprit. The smoke alarm continued to bleep intermittently, becoming increasingly insistent throughout the morning. Eventually, Dave changed the battery in the alarm and peace returned.

Coincidence? Of course, you could argue that it was. Smoke alarm batteries usually last between one and two years. I have no idea how long the battery had been in Mum's alarm, but to lose its battery power on the very last day of occupation, just when Dad's usual mode of communication had been disconnected was great timing, wouldn't you agree? It certainly gave us a lot of fun.

We talked about this afterwards and wondered who'd actually unplugged the doorbell and why? Maybe someone thought Mum would want to take the 'magic' chimes with her. She didn't.

Meanwhile, on arriving at the new apartment with the first vanload of furniture and boxes, we saw that although Mum had changed her mind about the gold carpet she and Dad had chosen, ordering a pale cream one instead, the original gold one had, in fact, been laid by mistake. Reluctantly, Mum accepted the new colour.

Over the next two days, as we worked hard on the apartment, hanging curtains, unpacking boxes and assembling furniture, we realised that because the walls were cream, and most of the furniture was pale in colour, the rich, deeper-coloured carpet actually looked sumptuous and warm. We all agreed that the paler colour would have looked bland by comparison and would have been the wrong choice.

Perhaps the 'mistake' wasn't a mistake at all, we wondered. Later, we reflected on the message that Dad had given to Dianne during the séance about Mum's imminent move; after spelling out part of the apartment's name, Dad had suggested: 'You'll be right soon; just go with the changes.'

'Top of the World'

Jacky: Two days after we moved Mum into her new apartment, I was working on an article about children's paranormal experiences for a new magazine called *Eternal Spirit*. I was excited because they'd asked to use a picture of me on the front. A cover girl – Dad would have loved that!

I needed a story to go with the piece, so decided to use Georgina's dream visitation (in which she and Dad had been sitting on a boat together), as it was still so fresh in my mind. No sooner had I finished the feature than Georgina walked into my study, crying hard. Naturally, I asked her what the matter was. She told me: 'I was listening to the radio when one of Granddad's favourite songs came on. It was The Carpenters singing 'Top of the World' – the song we played at his funeral. It made me think of Granddad, and made me cry . . . '

I pulled Georgina into my arms. Losing Granddad was hard for the children. Living so close to my parents, meant that the girls saw their grandparents several times a week. But the timing of this particular episode was not lost on me. Wasn't it great that the 1973 hit was playing at exactly that moment on the radio – just as I was writing up Georgina's dream visit? Did it mean something or not? Who knows? I can only tell you it's a good many years since I've heard that song played *anywhere* (other than at the funeral, of course). And strangely (or not), I haven't heard it again since.

I often wonder, are *we*, the bereaved, the only ones who hear 'our' song at any given time, while others hear a different tune? Many of my readers tell me how a significant song seems to be repeatedly played on the radio, or in shops they are visiting etc, and how this brings great comfort. Maybe spirits just manipulate it so that we 'tune in' at the appropriate moment?

I immediately told Georgina of the 'coincidence': 'I've just *literally* finished writing up your dream visit from Granddad for a magazine. I think he must have prompted me to use *your* experience in the first place.'

Higher Realms

Madeline: The gaps between the phenomena were growing longer, but they hadn't ceased completely.

In an early-morning dream on 30 April, I went to a 'celebration of life' given for the deceased husband of a friend. In the dream, I was in an auditorium filled with people. The guests were in steeply sloping wooden tiers. A lot of my family were there, even though they didn't know the deceased.

Mum was talking a lot and not listening to the speakers, who were discussing their memories of my friend's husband. I found myself having to 'shush' her.

As I looked around the auditorium, behind and high above me, off to my right I caught sight of Dad. I knew he was dead. I craned my neck for another glimpse, convinced I'd seen him sitting there, high up, then somebody would shift in their seat and I would lose sight of him.

I looked again and saw him sitting further along the same row, but a little nearer to me, almost behind me now. It was definitely him. I got quite excited, and then I notice the *other* him, still sitting in the original place. Two of him! They were also synchronised. The two Dads moved and turned at the same time.

The more I became aware of this, the clearer I saw him. I couldn't reach him, but was shown the 'Double Dad' image, so I wouldn't later dismiss it as a coincidence. This *wasn't* just a similar-looking face in the crowd. Afterwards, still in my dream, I was trying to tell Mum what I'd seen, but felt frustrated with her lack of real interest or acceptance.

Analysing all of this after waking up, I understood more of the symbolic meanings that Dad had brought me. Mum was on a lower level or tier than us; my sisters sat alongside me, one level higher. Perhaps we were more 'ready' for communication. It was difficult to say how 'high' Dad was, maybe seven or eight levels above us. Perhaps Mum was not ready to hear from Dad yet, not ready for afterlife communication? Was the gap between them too large for her to see him at this stage?

I felt bad about this, but couldn't alter the things I'd dreamed. The 'levels' of the auditorium were more obvious to me now, although they weren't when I was dreaming about them. Mum had been sitting with the other widow – the wife of the man whose life we were there to celebrate. She'd been talking quite loudly as the service began. *She was not listening.*

Mum hadn't yet had a dream visit from Dad; perhaps Dad was trying to explain why. Could Dad have been around her now, but she was as yet unable to see him? We hoped that as she moved through the worst of her grief, she would literally raise her 'vibrational level', enabling contact from other side. We'd have to wait and see.

As for my part in the dream, due to being hemmed in and trying not to draw attention to myself or be disrespectful, I'd been unable to reach Dad's level. Obviously, I couldn't reach Dad's level as he was dead. The way was barred. But were daydreaming, meditation, sleep and hypnosis other 'levels'? Being unconscious or in a coma can produce spiritual encounters too, perhaps taking you one 'tier' closer to the Spirit realms?

Strange Overlaps of Reality

The two identical Dads were, for me, not only *proof* that this was an other-worldly experience, but also a clear example that he could be in two places at the same time, or even all around, now that he was on the other side. It also seemed to be a way for him to tell us, 'Although I'm in different places at the same time, or my energy is split, this isn't *half of me* or *half of my energy*, but all of me in both places.'

This reminded me of a theory involving quantum mechanics. Quantum mechanics shows us the world is not how it seems. Quantum physics is the science of the 'very small'. It works with atoms, and smaller, at the subatomic level. Particles at this size do not follow the normal motion patterns we are used to. It calculates, among other things, strange overlaps of reality; parallel dimensions or universes, *and* objects being in two or more places at the same time. Fascinating!

We know we are limited in the way we can detect the reality of the outside world by the margins and parameters of our senses. Other creatures on Earth have more finely attuned senses than humans. For example, some insects can hear in the ultrasonic range, over two octaves *above* what the human ear can detect, and some animals, such as elephants, can hear in the infrasonic range. This means that because low frequencies travel further, elephants can communicate over long distances. A dolphin's hearing too is so acute that it can pick up an underwater sound from fifteen miles away.

Amazingly bees, bats, turtles and some birds use the Earth's magnetic field for navigation. Imagine having a built-in compass like that – you'd never lose your way again! The human eye can capture a tiny fraction of the colour spectrum, and we cannot see infrared or ultraviolet. Ultraviolet light *is* visible however, to many animals, including birds, fish and insects. Remarkably, the common goldfish can see *both* infrared and ultraviolet light. And even our sense of taste doesn't measure up: we have only nine thousand taste buds, compared to seventeen thousand in rabbits.

Our insight too is incomplete. No matter how developed our senses seem, we are still restricted by what we can comprehend. As John Hagelin, PhD, the American particle physicist, put it: 'We're living in a world where all we see is the tip of the iceberg ... the immense tip of a quantum mechanical iceberg.' In other words, there is so much more beneath the surface that we can't see, but it doesn't mean that it isn't all there. So, if *we* can't see, hear or detect some-thing, it clearly doesn't mean that it *doesn't* exist. It might simply be beyond our limited human sensory range; beyond our spectrum of sight and sound. Sometimes we can *sense* that someone is with us, other times, an inner knowing is enough.

Many leading scientists now believe in parallel universes. Energy can't be uncreated. Scientists have discovered that we are all made up of 'energy' and 'vibration' so we must con-tinue to exist in some form after physical death. Think of a spinning top, for example. It is a solid, tangible and visible thing. But when we spin it faster and faster, it begins to dis-appear before our very eyes. The movement or 'vibration' is at such a rate that our limited vision no longer perceives the object as solid at all. We can 'see' right through it. But it is still there!

Reality then is open to question; it is based merely on our perceptions, and as we have seen, these are limited indeed. There is so much more out there. We surely need to keep an open mind about possibilities beyond our everyday thinking. Life as we know it is simply an illusion; an illusion created out of our ability – or inability – to understand the world.

The Case for the Afterlife

As science continues to overturn our previously long-held convictions, it would be a mistake to hold on to earlier beliefs, simply because we have always held them. We truly have to be open to possibilities, even those that might seem incredible at first.

In his fascinating book, *A Lawyer Presents the Case for the Afterlife*, Victor Zammit, a former practising attorney, formally qualified in a number of university disciplines, writes:

'After many years of serious investigation I have come to the irretrievable conclusion that there is a great body of evidence which, taken as a whole, absolutely and unqualifiedly proves the case for the afterlife. I will not be arguing that the objective evidence has high probative value. Nor am I suggesting that this evidence be accepted beyond reasonable doubt. I am stating that the evidence taken as a whole constitutes overwhelming and irrefutable proof for the existence of the afterlife.'

Jacky: Dad was taking advantage of his ability to manipulate our perception; he was already a real expert at afterlife contact and soon he starting bringing along his friends . . .

Chapter 14

Over, but not out

And God said, 'Let there be light' and there was
light, but the Electricity Board said he would have
to wait until Thursday to be connected.

Spike Milligan

Jacky: The Saturday after moving day, the family met up for
a little party at Mum's new apartment.

We put on a DVD of an old Morecambe and Wise film, *Night
Train to Murder*, in which the two entertainers become
embroiled in a 1940s murder mystery when they take Eric's
niece under their wing. This hilarious comedy thriller was a perfect accompaniment to the champagne celebration as the niece
was regularly speaking to Uncle Eric! Also, given that we'd
always said that our Eric looked and acted like Eric Morecambe,
the DVD seemed an ideal way to include our late family in our
celebration.

The following morning, I received a text message from
Madeline. She had a dream visitation to report.

Looking Fantastic

Madeline: Although Nick had experienced dream visitations in the past (a deceased family friend was a regular for him), and so was no beginner, he had not, until now, had a dream visit from Dad. He told me:

'Ron walked into my dream from the left-hand side; his stick was clicking on the floor. He seemed fairly old. You know – how he looked when he died. He sat down opposite me.'

'Was there anyone else there?' I prompted, keen for more information.

'Charlotte arrived and sat down next to her granddad. She linked arms with him. Your mum was sitting next to Charlotte, but she was looking out the window and didn't notice that your dad had walked in. You were there too and *you* could see your dad. He was talking to us all.'

'Oh?'

'Yes, as Ron spoke to me, his face got younger and younger until he looked as he did around his mid-forties. He looked *bloody fantastic*, actually! He was really laughing and there was such vitality behind his eyes. He had more hair and all his teeth – really, really healthy.'

As we knew by now, Dad had obviously appeared to his son-in-law initially as an old man for the purpose of recognition, later becoming younger and full of vitality, to show off how he felt now.

Nick continued: 'Your dad asked how *my* mum and dad were; I was frightened of losing the 'link' and waking up, so I didn't speak much. I was aware that Ron was dead, and I figured that if I kept *really* still it might maintain the energy he'd created. I saw him so clearly. It was brilliant.'

Nick was thrilled finally to have a visitation from his much-loved father-in-law, and although he hadn't said much on this occasion, he felt certain that now Ron had been to see him once, he would come again. When I chatted to Jacky about this later, she said that talking to the deceased didn't usually affect the experience in any way, but Nick could have been close to waking, and something had alerted him to this fact.

Sometimes, when the energy is low, a spirit will appear in black and white, or when the spirit physically touches us in the visitation, they become momentarily invisible. Other times, they will show themselves only from the waist up, sitting down. Sometimes, a complicated scene is laid out, but if the energy is lower the scene is simpler; two plain chairs in an empty room, for example. Although none of these signs appeared during Nick's visit from Dad, perhaps the energy was low that night and Nick was aware of what he needed to do to maintain the connection.

Jacky: The commemorative bench bought from some of the money donated in Dad's memory was a brilliant idea. The bench would be perfect, placed right outside the main entrance of The Mews where Mum had her new apartment. The whole family would use it, and we'd see the plaque which Dave made, each time we visited. The engraving read:

RONALD HILL
1930–2008
GONE FISHING

We had a little celebration buffet and invited the residents to join us. After everybody had eaten, I stood up and gave a short speech before we all trotted downstairs, cameras and champagne glasses in hands.

I laid some flowers on the bench and then 'toasted' Dad.

A Day Out With Dad

John and I always spent at least one whole day together over the weekend and, as National Trust members, we loved to take a picnic to a nearby stately home, castle or beautiful garden. I'd often arrive home from these outings in a state of pure bliss.

On Sunday 11 May, we decided to drive to the coast, as the weather was still hot. We woke up early, but various things kept delaying us from leaving the house at the time we'd originally planned. By the time we'd packed our picnic lunch, it was already midday.

The drive was beautiful. We'd chosen a long route for an afternoon trip. On the way we would stop at Tattershall Castle in Lincolnshire – an incredible fifteenth-century red-brick tower with six floors.

We broke our journey about halfway with our picnic and, by the time we got to the castle, it was late afternoon. Surrounded by a moat, the castle was in excellent condition. There was a slight breeze on this very hot day and I stopped for a while to cool down, while John was looking around the ground floor of the castle. Suddenly, I heard a plane fly overhead. It was low in the sky, slow and noisy, and even though I knew nothing about planes, I realised this was something old, probably a war plane. I rushed inside the castle and called to John urgently, but his stroll was leisurely and by the time he made his way outside the plane was far away in the distance. Even so, it was close enough for John to recognise it and he told me it *was* a war plane – a

Hurricane Fighter – and one which had played a very important part in the Battle of Britain.

We decided to climb the steps to the top of the medieval castle which rises dramatically above the Lincolnshire countryside. The tower is over a hundred feet tall; now that's a lot of steps, so I took my time! About halfway up, we could hear the engines of not one plane but two. Rushing to the side of the castle to peek through the arrow slits, we saw the Hurricane again, this time joined by a Lancaster Bomber – the most successful bomber used in the Second World War. John explained that the planes were part of an exhibition group, called the 'Battle of Britain Flight' and that they were probably on their way back from a show. They were heading in the direction of the RAF Coningsby air base, close by.

'I'm going to the battlements on the top to see more clearly,' John shouted from the steps above me.

'Well, then I am too,' I called after him.

We both shot up the winding staircase. John got to the top quickly, but I was exhausted in the heat and slowed down on the floor below. I could hear both planes circling round again and had a very clear view from this lower level. Nevertheless, I decided I should walk all the way to the top. John seemed very excited at seeing the planes and I remember thinking that Dad would have loved to have seen them too. Then the Hurricane landed at the RAF base which was easy to see from our elevated position.

No sooner had I decided that Dad would have loved to share the experience, than I felt I was no longer alone. As I continued on to the top floor, I heard his voice coming from inside my head: 'There's no way I could have climbed all those stairs with my stick!' it said, loud and clear. 'And anyway, we can see the planes much clearer on this side of life.'

I heard his voice as plain as if he'd been standing next to me. But who was 'we'? Who was with me on the top of this tower? I looked over my head and the Lancaster Bomber was now flying directly towards the tower. I gasped in shock and delight as it flew *right* over our heads – it was really low. So low, in fact, I felt I could have reached out and touched it. Immediately, I felt overwhelmed with a sort of pride – pride for my country, pride for the service these planes had given and pride for the men who had flown them and fought in the war. Then came a sense of belonging; as though I was a part of this. But I wasn't. Why was I feeling like this? These feelings were not my own and I knew it. Where did they come from?

Almost as suddenly, as I asked myself these questions, I knew the answers. The 'energies', the '*we*' identified themselves. Dad was behind me with his arms on my shoulders – I felt them. Uncle Eric was to the right of me and my father-in-law Jack was to the left of me.

I could feel their very real sense of delight as the plane flew overhead and, just as quickly, I was surrounded by the most powerful love. It totally engulfed me, and then it overwhelmed me as each of these amazing men stepped into my personal aura, my energy field. I could 'feel' their personalities, and their love was like one massive hug, all of them surrounding me at once.

And then the tears came. It wasn't the thought of them being with me (I was happy about that), it was the *sense* of them – I was submerged in their affection, and the tears were theirs and mine intermingled. Then I heard Dad's voice again:

'Yes . . . timing is everything.'

And then I got it. No wonder John and I had wasted so much time in the morning. We'd been spiritually delayed! We had to be at the castle at this exact moment so that these three wonderful men could be watching as the planes flew over. Yes they'd come to visit *me,* but they'd been here to see the planes too, of course. I knew that Dad loved planes and so did Eric.

I cried and cried, thankful that I was wearing my dark sunglasses; thankful too that the crowds now gathered on the top of the castle were too preoccupied to wonder why this strange woman was bawling her eyes out.

Afterwards, I felt totally drained. Maybe from the tears or maybe something else? We'd chosen this 'random' spot for our day out – but it wasn't random at all. Everything had been organised by some higher power.

We decided to head off for the coast for a quick walk on the beach before returning home. As we got in the car, I chatted to John about what I'd experienced. Then he turned to me quietly and whispered.

'You knew my Dad was in the RAF, didn't you?'

I did know, I think, but I'd certainly forgotten. As soon as I got into the car I grabbed my bag to pick up my phone. Madeline had left me a text message so I rang her back. She would understand; and so she did. She too had been crying a few tears of her own. She'd been working on the book, writing down memories of our dear and darling father.

Madeline: It was early days to be writing a book about our wonderful father, with our grieving still so raw, but with so many phenomena being reported, we had to get the information down before it was forgotten. Both Jacky and I knew this was important. The sheer volume of experiences from so many different people meant this part of the book would be amazing, and we wanted to share as many of these incredible incidents as we could in the hope that others would find comfort in them.

We are lucky, I guess, because we talk about the after-life so openly in the family, readily swapping our spiritual stories with each other. I realised that other families must have experienced phenomena as we had, yet had, perhaps, been too frightened or too embarrassed to share their experiences.

Anyway, on this particular day, having cried too much to carry on writing, I went and sat in the garden for a break, and to enjoy the sunshine. Sam came out and gave me a hug. He asked what was wrong. I explained that Aunty Jacky and I had chosen a hard book to write emotionally.

I decided to send Jacky a text message telling her how I felt. She called me back and explained that she too had been crying – but in her case it was tears of joy. She'd felt incredible love and was overwhelmed by it. We'd both been crying at the same time, but speaking to her gave me the strength to keep going, knowing that Dad was enjoying a day out watching his favourite planes.

I know that Dad's around, and totally accept that his life has continued on a new and exciting level, but every piece of evidence, every 'coincidence' really helps me to settle and focus, enabling me to continue with the job of getting on with my own life – and writing up his book. Thanks Dad!

Jacky: John and I walked hand in hand along the windy beach, stopping only for John to write a message on the sand: 'JOHN LOVES JACKY XX', all wrapped up in a giant heart. He'd written my name on every beach around the world that he'd ever visited. I felt loved, cherished by the men in my life – on both sides of life.

I felt slightly 'spaced out' for two or three hours, but a cup of tea and a scone seemed to help – very grounding! And luckily for me, John drove all the way back.

As it wasn't too late, we called in on Mum on the way home. No sooner had I started to update Mum on the events of the day, than the table lamp in her apartment flickered. We laughed, joking that Dad was up to his old tricks again.

We began to chat about other things, but within about ten minutes we'd come full circle and were talking about what had happened that day again. The moment I mentioned the word 'castle', the lamp flickered for a second time, and this time Mum pointed it out first. As before, the conversation moved on, then twenty minutes later the subject came up once again. This time, I added in a little more detail I'd remembered and, once again, the lamp flickered on cue!

Coincidence? No way, I knew then for sure that Dad was listening in. We both did.

After all this time, we all wondered if the visitations might slow down a little, but we soon learned that Dad had other ideas . . .

Chapter 15

Man of the match

Any man can be a father, but it takes a
special person to be a dad.

Proverb

Just Checking In

Jacky: It was now the middle of May. Debbie was getting ready
for work one morning, when she felt Dad in the room. She told
us:

'I had a weird feeling, almost like Dad had popped in to see
me. I felt like he was worried about me because I was up so early
in the morning. I found myself reassuring him in my head and
telling him: I'm fine.'

'Why would he be worried about you?' I asked her.

'Because last time he came to visit me I'd been crying a lot.
But although I've been tearful since the funeral, I feel more
together now, as if I'm beginning to sort things out in my
head.'

Later, Debbie showed me her horoscope for that day. Like many people, we have our daily horoscope delivered by email each day. Also, like many people, we listen to the good predictions and ignore the bad ones! Debbie felt her horoscope reflected the visit from Dad. It read:

> ... visions could bring some amazing insights ... you might find them too off-the-wall to believe, but follow-up research could reveal [it] is actually quite credible. Keep a journal ... This might be useful to you later when you pass your ideas on to others ...

Debbie did just that; she passed her 'visions' on to me to write up.

Granddad's Lovely Scent

A couple of days later, Charlotte had a visitation dream from her Granddad. Even though she'd appeared in Nick's dream, this was the first dream she herself could recall consciously. I was sitting at my computer when she came in. 'Can I talk to you a minute, Mum?' she asked.

I turned to look at her and noticed her eyes were a little red, as if she'd been crying. 'What's the matter?' I asked soothingly, taking her hand.

'I had a dream about Granddad last night. All I remember is that I was dreaming and then I saw Granddad, so I walked over to him. I knew I was asleep and I knew he was dead.'

'How fantastic – this is your first visitation from Granddad then.'

'Yes. He hugged me Mum, and when I laid my head against

his chest I got such a loving feeling. The strangest thing was it *felt* just like Granddad and *smelled* just like Granddad.'

'You mean like Granddad's lovely aftershave that he always wore?'

'Yes. It was exactly the same. I felt like he was letting me know that *this* is the way we do it now. This is the way we meet, like when I'm asleep. I did get a sort of déjà vu – like we'd done this before and we were going to be doing it again in the future.'

'Do you remember Uncle Nick saw you in his dream visit?'

'Well, yes I remember you telling me about it, but I did feel Granddad had visited *me* before and I just never remembered it when I woke up. I knew it was his way of saying, "This is how it is; this is how it *has* to be"; and that he is still part of our lives and still helping us. It did make me cry though, Mum, because I realise how much I miss him. I talk to him all the time and I *did* feel like he was helping me. But now I know for sure.'

Just like Debbie, Charlotte felt that Granddad was 'passing through', as if he had work to do and was just 'calling in' on his way past. She took the opportunity to ask me about my research on afterlife contact and decided that she might finally read one of my books.

Although the girls were aware of my work in this field and I'd given them signed copies of all of my books, these had all ended up under their beds or in the attic, unread. Of course, this worked out for the best, because it meant they were not influenced by what I'd said might or could happen. Consequently, their experiences of their granddad in the afterlife are untainted and I have written exactly what they have told me here.

I now felt more than ever that Dad's visits were not 'random', and that some higher power was insisting that more people having contact with him meant more 'proof'.

Maybe Dad had visited others too? It would be interesting to find out, and later on Mum bumped into someone 'co-incidentally' who knew nothing about the book (or my work) ... but bizarrely, had still had a dream.

Fit and Well on the Other Side

A few days later, I was driving along in the car when I saw two of Dad's oldest friends in my mind's eye. Although Pat had died many years before, what surprised me was that Terry, her husband (who was like an uncle to me growing up), was with her in my vision. Terry had been seriously ill with Parkinson's for many years and now had Alzheimer's too. I hadn't seen him for over a year.

Later that day, I discussed my vision with Mum and several other family members. (Interestingly, Dianne and Dad visited this same couple in *her* dream.) I was worried. Had Terry passed over now too? Sure enough, a couple of days later, Mum had a phone call to say her dear friend Terry *had* actually died. In my vision, he'd looked well and was smartly dressed in a suit and tie; Pat was wearing a straight skirt and a fur coat. They looked radiant and happy. I wondered if they'd met Dad yet. Terry was too ill to be told that his friend Ron had died just a few weeks earlier. Imagine his surprise when his old friend Ron was there to greet him at the pearly gates!

Madeline: At the beginning of June Debbie and her husband went to a fortieth birthday party in Walsall. As it was quite a long drive, they decided to stay in a small hotel overnight.

During the party, Debbie met a lady who'd also recently lost her father. The other woman's grief encroached on Debbie's mood and, as the evening wore on, she began to feel upset about Dad.

Sitting alone quietly, she remembered 'Poppy', the name she'd chosen for a baby she'd miscarried fifteen years earlier. She inwardly mourned both her losses, but not wanting to disrupt the party, she discreetly wiped her tears away. She eventually allowed herself to enjoy the evening a little and dance. Others at the party noticed she was a little quiet, but they didn't comment.

Later that night, Debbie had a dream visitation. Dad appeared to her, but didn't say a word. He was holding a tiny baby in his arms. She was swaddled in a small pink flannelette sheet, and Dad was gazing at her with the sort of smile he reserved for his grandchildren. Debbie knew immediately that this was Poppy. It was the second time she'd seen the blonde, curly-haired, blue-eyed baby; the first time was in another dream when she was with our grandmother – Mum's mother.

Debbie already knew our grandmother was looking after Poppy and now saw that Dad was too. I think it also shows that our loved ones on the other side of life can be very aware of our trials and tribulations and our thoughts and worries on this side. Had Dad tuned in to Debbie's sad evening? It seemed possible.

Happy Father's Day

Jacky: Sunday 15 June – Father's Day. Our first one.

I hadn't remembered when I woke up that morning. The girls had both 'texted' John a Father's Day message each – the modern way. *Be nice, do more* . . . I thought. *You have a father and I don't* . . . Words I couldn't and didn't say out loud. Yet they'd done nothing wrong; teenagers who'd both remembered Father's Day was a good thing. I was cross at anyone and everything and they didn't deserve my internal rage. John and I went out for a late-afternoon meal together. I felt the need to spoil my husband, as I couldn't treat my father. John became my substitute – my stand-in 'Dad' for the day. With no one to buy a card or present for, I felt empty, sad.

Later, I popped to the village stores. They were full of people buying beer and Father's Day cards. I had to gulp back the tears, something I hadn't anticipated. Thank goodness it was a sunny day, so I was wearing my life-saving dark sunglasses again!

I've never believed in remembering 'special days' after losing someone. Surely every day was sad, wasn't it? Why would one be more sad or more special than another? But this belief came back to haunt me as I realised that today – Father's Day – *did* hurt just a little bit more.

Traditionally, a visit to my parents on this day would have been on the agenda. Although Mum was away, having chosen to visit family for a short break, I decided to call round to the apartment anyway. The bench – Dad's bench – was outside and I'd be able to sit there.

I'd never believed in taking flowers to a graveside either, yet on this day I found myself with the same needs as every other grieving human being. I wanted a ritual, something to mark the day with – a place to visit Dad and talk to him. Believing in an afterlife helps a lot, but it doesn't cover every eventuality. Dad was here, *everywhere*, in fact, but I couldn't hug him today and I missed that.

I tied a single white rose from the garden to Dad's bench instead and, strangely enough, it helped. I felt I was doing it for all of us. 'Happy Father's Day, Dad. I love you,' I whispered; and I swear he whispered back, but I didn't *feel* him. Where was he today?

Gone Fishing

Madeline: I didn't even acknowledge that it was Father's Day and my father-in-law got entirely overlooked.

Tony had kindly arranged to take his grandsons, Sam and Jim, fishing for the day. Neither of the boys had ever fished before, and they were unsure what to expect. There was a charity competition on and over thirty kids entered, including Sam and Jim.

As luck would have it, Jim caught the first fish of the day, and was delighted. Flushed with beginner's success, Jim later said, 'Granddad was helping me!' and we all agreed. Sam went on to catch the biggest carp (Granddad's favourite fish) and was duly awarded 'Fisherman of the Day'. He won a fishing rod – the first he'd ever owned.

Sam agreed with Jim that they hadn't been alone on the riverbank that day, and the boys talked about it excitedly with their Gramps in the car on the way home.

So both Gramps *and* Granddad had spent Father's Day with their grandsons. And I couldn't think of anywhere Dad would rather have been on a sunny June day than down on the riverbank with his grandsons, catching carp.

Dad had been an award-winning fisherman; in fact, his pitch on the River Windrush was affectionately known as Ron's Hole. He could have taught his grandsons so many angling tips and secrets; they could have gained so much from his years of experience, and he would have loved their new-found enthusiasm. Sadly though, the boys took up this hobby four months after his passing – four months too late. But was it too late? Dad clearly wasn't going to let a small thing like being dead interfere with his influence down on the riverbank. After all, I reflected – what were the chances of *both* boys really having such amazing beginners' luck?

I called Mum later to tell her where Dad had spent the day. She was delighted to hear about it, and to learn of the boys' success on their first fishing trip.

I wouldn't normally have called Mum while she was away, but I was glad I had. She told me she'd had a difficult morning. She'd been sleeping in a double bed for the first time since losing Dad and had woken up feeling disorientated. She'd reached across for him and, finding the bed empty, had wondered if he was in the bathroom. Then suddenly, fully awake, she'd remembered that he was no longer alive. Just for a moment though, she'd been caught out; she'd forgotten, and it had made her sad all over again.

We wondered if Dad *had* been with her in the night, his spirit at least. And if Mum had woken to feel that Dad was suddenly missing, was she getting closer to being aware of his presence? Did she unknowingly *sense* him being there? Perhaps 'remembering' him visiting was now only a matter of time for her. Of course, if Mum was upset by the experience, Dad would naturally hold back before attempting something similar again. His presence was supposed to be a comfort, after all.

Our Own Communication

Jacky: As part of my research, I'd studied spirit-communication tools, including Ouija boards and séances. I'd learned as much as I could about these types of communication, not only so that I could write about them objectively in my books, but also to know and understand how to perform a séance safely. I didn't give mediumistic readings to other people in my work; even though it was something I'd experienced myself on many occasions.

As a family, it seemed that many of us had mediumistic and psychic abilities, and we never had any trouble reaching out to the other side in this way. So we'd decided to conduct our own séance in my pretty conservatory at home, surrounded by the angel figurines I collect and love. Dianne is a medium too and often works with a local spiritualist church as a volunteer reader. Debbie had experienced many episodes of clairvoyance, as well as dream visitations. Between us, with our experience and knowledge, we felt competent.

We'd decided to use a tool called an Angel board. Decorated with beautiful images of angels, this was much like a traditional Ouija board with letters in a circle around the outside, the difference between the two being the *intent*. The intent (always the most important thing in any séance) was to communicate using the highest possible channel. So the words, 'Is anybody there?' were never used at *our* séances. Pauline, as a professional Medium, was also very careful and asked to speak to Spirit Friends. We only talked to our loved ones or to angel guides and had no interest in chatting with just anyone.

Forget darkened rooms and scary ghosts – we were sitting in full daylight, a pretty scented candle was burning and flowers from the garden decorated the room. Dianne, Debbie and I were now ready to make contact with Dad . . . if *he* was willing to contact *us*!

After saying a prayer, we followed a practised ritual of protection from negative or uninvited entities. Then, prayers and preparations in place, we set about contacting 'the other side'.

'If that really is you Dad, prove it,' I said, looking heavenwards. And the séance began. After an initial dodgy start, where the pointer seemed to spell out nonsense, we finally made a connection:

Jacky, Debbie & Dianne (J, D & D): Is that you, Dad?
Murmurs of cautiously optimistic excitement.
Dad: YES.
J, D & D: Can you spell out your name?
Dad: RON.
More excitement – then concern.
J, D & D: Where is Mum?
Dad: MEWS.
J, D & D: Yes, where is that? *Dad spelled out correctly the name of the village where he and Mum had lived for about thirty-six years and the name of Mum's new apartment.* Are you on your own or is someone with you?
Dad: PETER.
No one appears to have asked who this was, but he explains about a guide later on.
J, D & D: Where are you in the room?
The pointer shot over to a space by the wall. We then asked if he could make a sound but no sound came. No tapping or knocking was heard throughout the session even though the pointer had spelled out YES; he seemed unable to create a psychic knocking sound.
J, D & D: *In a fun voice:* How the devil are you? *Giggles.*
Dad: AOK. GOOD.
J, D & D: *More laughter and joyful noises.*
Who else is with you?

Dad: YOU!

J, D & D: *More laughter.* Anyone else

Dad: JUST A GUIDE.

J, D & D: *More muttering as we discussed the fact that we assumed he would have appeared with his brother Eric. Then we were stumped as to what to ask next. Our darling dad had travelled through many dimensions to reach us and we couldn't think of a single thing to say. Then we had a plan. Perhaps he could enlighten us on his journey? Then*: Can you tell us what happened when you died?

Dad: YES.

J, D & D: Was it like you showed us in the dreams?

Dad: YOU KNOW . . .

Of course, he'd shown his journey or parts of his journey to several people in different ways.

J, D & D: So what we've seen in dreams is what happened to you?

Dad: YES.

J, D & D: So you didn't go through a tunnel of light then?

Dad: NO.

At this point, Debbie recalls her dream where he shows her how he left his body after a single pain. And Georgina had said after his one sharp pain, he'd woken up on the other side about a week later (in his frame of reference) and he was OK – dead, but OK.

We also remembered Madeline telling us about the drive up from Cornwall on the night Dad died and seeing the monument resembling a tunnel of light. If Dad did have missing time, of course, he may have passed along this tunnel of light on the night he died, but didn't recall it. We'll never know.

Although many people expect this to happen, the 'tunnel' experience is, in fact, present in less than one third of cases.

J, D & D: Were you given a choice – to come back or not?

Confused spellings with no clear meanings. No answer given here; probably just as well. We asked another question: Who did you see first when you got there?

Dad: DAD.

J, D & D: Oh my God. That must have been amazing! *Dad hadn't seen his father for a great many years; as he was only two years old when his father died, he may not even have remembered him. Much 'oohing' and 'aahing', then:* Who was next?

Dad: ERIC, MUM …

J, D & D: Then who was next?

Dad: DOG. *The pointer continued to spell …* LOTS OF DOGS. OZ. *Oz was a much-loved pet who'd belonged to Debbie. We were all surprised that Dad was met by dogs!* EIGHT DOGS.

J, D & D: *More mumbles of surprise.* What happened next, Dad?

Dad: ERIC. TAKE …

J, D & D: Eric took you somewhere?

Dad: ON A BOAT WITH DAD, NAN *[the name for our mother's mum]*, MUM *[his mum]*, DENNIS *[we had no idea who this was – another guide maybe]*, ANNE *[a deceased family friend]*.

J, D & D: *At this point we realised this was going to be a very long list so we decided to ask another question:* Where did you go?

Dad: NERJA.

This was Dad's favourite Spanish holiday location. Yet it was also where he'd been taken ill with his gallstones; the bad memories were obviously forgotten now. Perhaps he was taking his afterlife family on a guided tour, showing them the delights they'd missed in life. Next, Dad shared some personal information about our lives.

Later Dad spelled out the words 'van driver' and we didn't know what this meant. Was the unknown 'Dennis' the 'van driver' who'd been with him at the time of his accident so many years before? Or was this something else? Mum didn't know either, when we asked her later. This query was left unanswered and we still haven't figured it out.

J, D & D: Will you be visiting Mum in a dream Dad? *Even though most of us had experienced dream visits by this time, Mum still hadn't and we wondered why.*

Dad: TOO SOON 4 SOME.

J, D & D: *Dad had been communicating for nearly an hour now and the communication was still strong. Even we were tired by this time. How had he managed to stay in our 'atmosphere' for so long and bring such clear messages? We asked:* How come you can manage to stay so long Dad?

Dad: I LOVE YOU.

J, D & D: *We were barely holding it together by this time. The session was becoming so real, so intimate – so sad, yet so happy. There was a moment's silence as we pulled ourselves together, before asking*: But you will visit Mum when the time is right?

Dad: YES. TELL HER I LOVE HER.

At this point we sisters let go of the pointer, tears filled our eyes, and when we placed our fingers back on again, it spelled out a final short message.

Dad: BYE X.

But of course, it wasn't really goodbye now, was it?

Chapter 16

Visiting hours

Dying is a very dull, dreary affair. And my advice
to you is to have nothing whatever to do with it.

W. Somerset Maugham

Madeline: In May, Nick had his second dream visitation. This
time, the setting for the visit was an old house of Mum and
Dad's; once inside though, the layout was different from how
it had been in real life.

Dad was at the top of the stairs, with a towel wrapped
around his middle, going towards the bathroom for a shower.
Nick was aware that Dad had died, but decided not to men-
tion it or draw attention to it, in case it brought him out of the
dream. As before, he was excited but cautious, wanting to
prolong the experience for as long as possible. I think this
shows how lucid he actually was during the experience. He
noted that Dad looked younger and 'fit as a flea'.

Nick was aware that Mum was downstairs in the 'dream'
house, which seemed really untidy and cluttered. She was

busy tidying, and he felt she was aware of Dad's presence, but was too busy to pay it much attention. He recalled: 'I was holding the small Masonic penknife – the bottle opener that your dad had shown Jacky in *her* dream; I felt that Debbie had borrowed it, and I sensed that she was downstairs somewhere. I don't know why, I never saw her.'

'Hang on a minute, let me write this down,' I interrupted. 'OK, what happened next?'

'I called up to him, "Here you are Charlie", and began to walk up the stairs towards him, to hand over the penknife. I got almost to the top step. He didn't come down. I didn't quite reach your dad's level, but handed the penknife up to him. I was aware and surprised that I could climb nearly to the top to meet him.'

'Surprised because you were close to his "spiritual level"?' I asked Nick.

'Yes, there seemed some significance to the fact I'd been able to do this. Your dad looked at the knife and said, "That's a bloody cracker," [a common phrase of his relating to something which gave him joy] and he seemed really pleased to have it back. Then your dad started laughing his head off about something, although I don't remember what, and I was laughing with him.'

'That's lovely! So was that the end?'

'Well, then I walked downstairs but had to climb back over all the clutter to get to the room below. Next, I went outside, still in my dream. There was a lot more clutter and I thought it was weird.'

Working through the dream bit by bit, I wondered whether the reason Dad was wearing only a towel was so that he could show Nick how physically fit he was now. With regard to the clutter, Mum's apartment is actually immaculate, so we felt it must have a spiritual meaning – maybe her mind was too 'full' at the moment, but she was 'clearing' it in life, as she was in the dream. Debbie was downstairs in the dream too; was she clearing her own cluttered thoughts, or helping Mum to clear hers?

Nick described being surprised to find that he could climb so high on the stairs – perhaps it was because he meditated nearly every night. As for the penknife/bottle opener, Jacky later suggested that Dad had needed this back because we'd used it to celebrate his life and now he had some celebrating of his own to do, on the other side.

It was wonderful that Nick and Dad were laughing together, as they'd often done in life. In the dream Nick actually called Dad by his nickname 'Charlie', as if to clarify the earlier confusion over who Charlie was at Dianne's séance.

Health Caution Comes True

I phoned Mum a couple of days later for a chat. We spoke once or twice every week, sometimes for an hour or more. I thought this would be an ordinary call to catch up with each other's news.

'Hi Mum,' I said. 'What are you up to?'

'I'm sat in the chair,' she told me. 'Actually, I don't feel very well.' She sounded strange; I picked up the stress in her voice.

I sat upright in my armchair. 'What's the matter?' I asked.

I just feel awful. I've got a doctor's appointment in an hour.'

'Maybe you have a virus,' I suggested.

Mum was rarely ill, and when she was it was usually a chest infection. She didn't sound chesty though.

'Maybe. Look, I'd better go,' she said.

I felt she was rushing me off the phone, which was most unusual. 'Well, let me know how you get on.'

An hour and a half after Mum's appointment I rang her again. There was no answer.

Jacky: The phone rang and it was Mum. I was surprised to hear her voice as I'd been with her just a few hours before.

'Now I don't want to worry you, and I don't want you to rush in,' she began.

This immediately alerted me. 'Now I don't want to worry you ...' This was what she'd always said when Dad was ill. But it'd been over three and a half months since Dad had died. Why was she saying it now?

'Where are you,' I asked. 'Is everything OK?'

'I'm in Burton hospital.'

'What's happened?' I assumed that she'd fallen and broken something. I couldn't believe it. After years spent following Dad around hospitals, Mum had now been admitted too.

Mum explained, 'I felt my heart racing, so I rushed to the doctor. I didn't even lock the apartment door. I might not have closed it ... The doctor insisted on calling an ambulance. I didn't even bring my mobile; I've bumped into an old friend in the hospital and he's lent me his phone. I might have to stay in. Could you pack a bag and bring in the usual?'

'The usual' – yes, I'd done this a few times before: bag, tooth-brush, toothpaste, night clothes. I went through the list in my mind ...

The old friend Mum had mentioned was John – someone she had worked with a long time ago, but hadn't seen in ten years. She described how John had approached her at the hospital and held out his hand ready to shake hers, his face a mixture of shock and happiness at seeing his old friend. Then he'd said sadly, 'We were sorry to hear about Ron. I was away on a business trip and didn't hear about the funeral until after I'd returned. Strange though – I had a dream about him the other night.'

Mum began to explain to John why *she* was in hospital, and he lent her his phone so that she could call me. But Mum was intrigued about what John had told her. She had to find out more about the dream, but just as she was about to ask John for more detail, she was called in to see the doctor. John quickly passed Mum his business card as she was wheeled away on her trolley.

Was Dad now visiting people outside our immediate group of friends and family, she wondered? And if this was a visitation from Dad, it was a clever plan. We couldn't wait to find out . . .

Madeline: Twenty minutes after I'd got no reply from Mum's phone, our landline rang. It was Jacky: 'Mum's in hospital, she just rang me.'

'But I only spoke to her earlier. What happened?' I was struggling to understand.

'She went to the doctor and they called an ambulance. The doctor obviously wasn't happy with her, Madeline, but she told me she feels fine now and a bit of a fraud. They're doing some tests, but I'm going in anyway. Mum thinks they might let her go home this afternoon.'

This was reassuring, but still, it was the last thing I'd been expecting. 'OK,' I said. 'Let me know as soon as you find out any more.'

'Will do,' she replied.

Jacky kept me informed throughout the evening, as she'd promised. The last phone call was at half-past midnight. Jacky was just leaving the hospital; they were keeping Mum in overnight after all.

Jacky: 'A heart attack?' My disbelief was clear. After years spent sitting by Dad's bedside, Mum, the fit one, was now in hospital following a heart attack!

'Yes, sorry about that!' said Mum, looking sheepish, as if it was somehow her fault.

My sisters and I were all lying half-asleep on Mum's hospital bed, while she sat up in a chair, hair and make-up perfect. I took photographs on the camera I always carry in my bag and laughed later when I looked at the shots. Mum looked great; we looked awful – exhausted!

Despite the worry though, we all remained calm as we joked about my dream visit from Dad a few weeks earlier. In the dream, Dad had showed me Mum lying in a hospital bed. We'd laughed about it at the time, as Mum had appeared to be in perfect health and we'd had no idea this was coming. Dad had warned me that the hospital might suggest it was something serious, but we were not to worry; she was going to be fine, with many more years yet to live.

In hindsight, Dad's warning was the best thing he could have done. Coming so shortly after his death, Mum's heart attack could have pushed the family over the edge – the family who up until that point had been holding it all together so well. Dad couldn't stop the heart attack, and indeed, it was probably a life lesson of some sort, but he could – and did – minimise the trauma of the whole thing.

How Are They Aware of What Happens in Our Lives on Earth?

Dad indicated several times that not only was he aware of what was happening in our lives but also that he was able to see 'slightly ahead', into our future.

He didn't know about everything though, and on more than one occasion when we asked a question he said he would 'find out', meaning he had to go and check a reference somewhere, perhaps in the so-called 'Book of Life'. Many people see 'their life flash before their eyes' at the point of physical death (we know this from reports of near-death experiences). Is this the reference he uses to check on our own future happenings? At the point of death do we also 'tune in' to the 'Book of Life'?

Some see an actual book which records all of our deeds, thoughts and actions during our lifetime (you can look into the future as well as into the past). Others see a type of movie screen of life which they can view or enter into (there are other variations). All this is available on 'the other side' and some psychics believe that this is the source that they too are able to review to enable them to give psychic readings/predictions.

According to P. M. H. Awater, author of *The Big Book of Near-Death Experiences,* about 30 per cent of adult near-death experiencers report having seen the 'Book of Life' during their near-death episode.

The Gift of Vitality

After the heart attack, we felt that more than ever Mum was now replacing Dad as the object of our care and attention. Her heart *hadn't* actually stopped, but *had* been under enormous stress. It was still a heart attack the doctors said; the tests proved it.

Three days after Mum was released from hospital with an enormous bag of tablets, I took another photograph of her. We were sitting in a coffee shop and she was wearing a pink sweater and matching cardigan. She looked beautiful, serene and at total peace with the world. It was the prettiest I had ever seen her and we each printed a copy of the picture for our own photograph albums.

Mum wasn't going anywhere, but we were reminded that as our only remaining parent she was a very precious package indeed, and we resolved to take very good care of her!

After Mum told us about her friend, John's, dream I decided to email him. He replied a few days later on his return from another trip away, and I called him for a chat.

John's dream followed a pattern similar to the one we'd all experienced, but because he'd had no clue that Dad had already visited many family members and friends in dreams, plus he hadn't even seen Mum or Dad for years, this isolated visitation was great validation for us. Note that during the dream John is aware that Dad is dead – a classic 'visitation' sign. This is what John told me:

'I was really sad about the loss of my old friend and also disappointed to have missed the funeral. I had the dream a couple of nights later.

'The dream was quite a simple one, but seemed very real at the time. I was at a gathering of people and Ron was there. In the dream, I knew that Ron had died and that maybe the people who were with him had died too. Maggie was also there.

'Ron was standing up, but your mum was sitting in an unusual way. She was upright, but her feet were straight out in front of her; sitting on something, but not on a chair – I didn't know *what* it was. When I woke up, I was very moved by the experience and I was actually crying with sadness. That morning, I told my wife about the dream, as well as several friends, because it was so powerful and clear.

'Imagine then how stunned I was to see Maggie just a few days later at the hospital. We'd taken a family member in to the emergency department; luckily, she was not as poorly as we'd expected. When it was time to leave, we headed towards the exit, but noticed that another set of double doors was open, so we changed our minds and decided to cut across the waiting room and go out that way instead. It was *then* that we saw Maggie.

'I had the strangest feeling of déjà vu when I saw her. She was actually sitting on a trolley waiting to see a doctor – she was sitting just as I'd seen her in my dream, upright with her feet in front of her! The way we bumped into Maggie at the hospital seemed a real coincidence.'

When John had finished, I said to him, 'That's just brilliant – and let me tell you why.' I then gave John a summary of what had been happening to other family members. He was astounded.

Madeline and I found it interesting that so many people were using the phrase déjà vu to describe their dreams or the experiences that followed, as if triggering a memory. Déjà vu – causing you to believe you are remembering something that has previously happened, a *real* experience, like Mum sitting on the trolley.

John's dream visitation was an extremely emotional occurrence for him, to the extent that he'd actually woken up crying and felt compelled to share his dream, not only with his wife but with other friends as well. Let's face it, it's highly unusual for most people to even *remember* their dreams in such detail, let alone share them with others.

Can you imagine what it took for the spirits 'upstairs' to arrange that these two people would be in the same physical space within days of the dream, after all those years?

What had made John and his wife take the longer route out of the hospital? Only by taking this different route, would they run into Mum. And thankfully, the relative that they'd taken into hospital didn't turn out to be seriously ill, after all; could it be that the whole episode was a spiritual ploy to get these people together?

Although I had no proof, I always felt that Dad had been with his afterlife friends and relatives at the hospital, healing Mum in some way. Maybe that is why she looked so well – positively glowing – just a couple of days later when I took her photograph.

Dad had delivered a master stroke this time. He'd started to widen his circle, bringing messages now to people we hadn't seen in a long time – people who knew nothing about other dreams and visitations or the book. And he wasn't finished yet . . .

Chapter 17

Because death is not the end

Truth is stranger than fiction, but it is because
Fiction is obliged to stick to possibilities; Truth
isn't.

Mark Twain

Jacky and Madeline: If any of our family had doubts about
an afterlife at the beginning of these experiences, then they
certainly hadn't by the time we'd written the book. Writing
them down and looking at them individually helped to clarify
and illuminate them, showing just how special they really
were. Because we both made notes and caught all the occur-
rences as and when they happened, it meant that we missed
nothing; and even if we didn't consider particular details
important at the time, subsequent events often proved that
they were.

Drawn to Visit

Jacky: Driving back from the gym one day, I felt the urge to visit my old friend Sally. Sally and I had known each other our whole lives and lived just a minute's walk away from each other. I couldn't remember the last time I'd 'spontaneously' called at her house; it had to be at least a year ago or longer. Yet this day I felt drawn to her.

After spending an hour together chatting generally and drinking tea, it appeared that there was, after all, no pressing reason for my visit. Confused, I went home. I'd been convinced that Dad had led me to her door.

A few weeks later, after Madeline and I had been working non-stop on the book, we decided to take a day off. I made plans to spend the day with another friend, Sue, whom I had met several years earlier through reiki healing classes.

A Vision of Friends

Sue came to pick me up. She had an exciting day planned for us, but first we stopped at the petrol station. As Sue went in to pay, I immediately had a vision of Dad with his recently deceased friend Terry. I saw the two of them clearly, but just from the waist up. Dad and Terry were smiling and laughing together – classic 'Dad'. The image appeared in the left-hand side of my vision, almost as if it were being projected out of my left eye, right in front of me. So they *had* met up! The last time I'd had a vision in this same way, Terry had appeared with his wife Pat – and we'd later discovered this was the day he died. Was I learning a new psychic skill? Were they *teaching* me a new skill? Was this a form of clairvoyance? What a great start to the day!

Sue got back in the car and we drove to a crystal warehouse.

It was exciting to be surrounded by the beautiful stones and I felt energised by them. Sue was admiring some crystal lamps and asked my opinion as to which she should purchase. I placed my hands around one which had caught my eye and said, 'This one's perfect; it has a lovely energy.' As I spoke, a small crystal fragment seemed to appear out of mid-air and land on the shelf right next to the lamp. This white crystal chip was bright in comparison to the soft pink glow of the lamp.

We were stunned. The owner had been right there with us and both Sue and he made a joke about it. I laughed along with them and looked upwards. Where had the fragment appeared from? There were no shelves above this one and the next 'stop' up was the ceiling.

'Was that something to do with you?' Sue asked me, laughing.

'I guess so,' I answered in surprise. 'It's probably Dad!'

After lunch, the pair of us visited a beautiful New Age store which was full of delights: candles, crystal jewellery, angel figurines and all manner of wonderful things. I went home feeling very uplifted.

The following week, I decided to make a display of my own beautiful crystals, but first I had to clear some clutter. Sorting through boxes of New Age music, inspirational books, and so on, I decided it was time to move some of it on. I emailed a few friends, including Sally who I'd impulsively visited a few weeks earlier, to see if they were interested in any of the items I no longer wanted. Sally rang me the next day and asked if she could call round.

A New Goodbye From Dad

When Sally arrived, she seemed excited. 'I think I know why you called at my house the other week,' she began.

'You do?' I asked, intrigued.

'Well, I remembered that a few days after your dad's funeral, my dad had a dream about *your* dad.'

'He did?' I was keen to hear more.

'Well, I don't remember much and I think it was a very short dream,' she began.

I picked up the phone and handed it to her: 'Ring your dad now,' I urged, impatient for the full story.

Sally's dad, another John, was married to Daphne (for whom Dad had 'rung' the doorbell, when she'd telephoned, shortly after his passing). Had Dad decided to get in touch with *this* John too to say goodbye?

Sally spoke to her dad, then passed me the phone. Bemused at my request, he began to recount his dream of months before.

'It was just a short dream,' he began. 'I was standing on a tree-lined road and your dad drove along in his old Granada. He was on his way fishing.'

'That sounds like Dad,' I interrupted.

'He wound down the window and we had a chat – general stuff. He asked me how *I* was and I asked him how *he* was. He said he was fine; and Jacky – he was really happy! And that was it, really. It wasn't frightening or anything. It was kind of nice, actually. I knew it was definitely your dad; there's no doubt about it. The dream was so clear and vivid!'

'Did you know that other people have had dreams like this?' I asked John.

'No,' he replied.

'Did you think it was different from other dreams you've had?'

'Well, yes – I told Daphne in the morning, and then Sally later. There was one thing that was strange though.'

'Yes?' I enquired.

'I recognised the road we were on. It was the road where I grew up; where I used to live when I was nine years old – when *my* dad died.'

And then I realised. Dad had something in common with his old friend. They'd both lost their fathers as young boys. How very sad. Dad had taken people to familiar places before – old haunts. Maybe he'd created this road memory especially for John? And how brilliant that he was driving his favourite car and about to go fishing.

Afterwards, Sally told me, 'I remember when Dad told me about his dream. I asked him if he knew Uncle Ron was dead in the dream and he said yes.'

So the dream fit the visit profile perfectly: John realised Dad was dead; the dream was clear and vivid; he recalled details like the car and the fishing trip; and the dream had moved him enough that he felt it worthy of sharing when he awoke. No wonder I'd felt drawn to visit Sally a few weeks earlier. Dad clearly wanted this story in the book.

Finally . . . Goodbye to Mum

It was the day after Sally's visit and I couldn't wait to tell Mum all about it. Sitting down over a cup of tea I began, 'So, Sally came round, and guess what? John's had a visitation!' Mum looked up surprised.

'Yes, isn't it amazing?' I continued, triumphant at this latest addition to our-ever growing file. 'There are over twenty people now who've had some paranormal experience relating to Dad.'

Mum smiled at me coyly, then said: 'Make that twenty-one.'

'No way!' I gasped, immediately understanding her meaning. 'You've *seen* Dad?'

'Yes,' she nodded. 'At last.'

I was now beside myself with excitement. 'Tell me. Tell me,' I begged. But then I quickly changed my mind, and said, 'No. Let me tell you about John's visit first.' I wanted to save Mum's experience – the one we'd all longed for – until last. So I explained about John's dream visitation, and then Mum told me hers. But it wasn't at all what I'd expected:

'It was only a short dream,' Mum began. (We'd heard that before!) 'In the middle of the night, I felt someone sit down on the bed and it woke me up. At least I thought I was awake. So I opened my eyes – and your dad was sitting on the end of the bed. I could see him clearly, because ... you know how the light shines through the curtain from the courtyard outside.'

'That's right,' I confirmed. 'It does.'

'I recognised him immediately. He was wearing that blue-patterned, cream sweater – the one he's wearing in that picture,' she said, pointing to a photograph she had on display.

'Oh yes, I remember it.'

'The colours were so vivid – really bright! Well, I was surprised. Why was he wearing clothes in the middle of the night? I said, "Hello." I was so pleased to see him. Then I leaned over to the lamp and switched it on; as soon as I put the light on, and looked back to where he was sitting, he was no longer there. It was only then that I thought, "Oh he's dead", but then I realised that this must be a "visitation", and was cross with myself that I'd switched the light on. It might have lasted longer if I hadn't.'

'No,' I reassured her. 'It probably wouldn't have made any difference. I expect it was only ever going to be a very short visit, being the first time. Maybe longer next time, eh?' I jumped up and down in my seat, excited for her. 'What happened then?' I asked.

'Well I just went right back into a lovely deep sleep. I felt really happy and contented.'

So Mum had her visit after all. It was six months since Dad had passed – six months before he was able to reach his grieving widow. But he'd done it now, and just in time to make the end of the book!

As before, we looked carefully at the experience and decided that Mum *must* have been awake; how else would she have switched on the light? She actually *felt* him sit on the bed, and this woke her up, the *physical* sensation.

Dad had experienced difficulties in reaching out to Mum in a dream state, so had chosen a new way to show that he was around her; this was only the second time he'd appeared in this physical form (the first being to his granddaughter Georgina at the bottom of the stairs – when she'd thought he was a burglar).

As he'd done on nearly every visitation, Dad had picked familiar clothing in which to appear to Mum. Was he aware of the few photographs Mum had chosen to display in her new apartment? It seems more than a coincidence that he'd been wearing the sweater in the photograph – a picture which was now several years old. Had he picked this image so she'd have a visual reference later, a photograph of him wearing exactly what she'd seen? Or had he chosen it because it was a sweater she loved to see him in – that shade of blue which suited him so well?

In the semi-darkness it seems important that he picked something which she would recognise immediately as 'Dad'. Had he worn a suit, or something less familiar, her reaction on seeing someone in her room might have been quite different. She might have screamed, as Georgina had initially, before spotting the walking stick. But with that sweater there was no mistaking the visitor!

So even 'brief visits' are carefully worked out in advance, it seems. And although Mum had been momentarily confused when she first woke up, she soon realised this had been real. Dad's visit comforted and consoled her, enabling her to fall into a deep, contented sleep . . . at last.

After discussing this latest visit, we believed that Dad may have attempted something similar before. We recalled Mum describing how she'd woken up in the double bed when staying at family friends, surprised to discover Dad 'missing'. She was upset *then*. This time, however, there was no doubt. This had been an authentic visit, not a confused dream.

Truth really is stranger than fiction.

Afterword

Jacky: In dream visitations, Dad tells us that he lifted out of his body after his heart attack. His soul separated from his physical body at the point of death.

Dad has said that his brother Eric was there to meet him when he arrived on the other side, and we'd all expected this, but what no one anticipated was that his father, who'd died when Dad was just two years old, was the first one to greet him when he went through the pearly gates.

We are met by the most important people in our lives. After Dad saw his closest relatives (father, mother, brother and his spirit guide), he showed both Dianne and I (in dream visitations) how he'd been greeted by crowds of friends and relations, who were literally queuing up to meet up with him again. It could be described as a 'welcome home party' in heaven. What a wonderful thought. Dad was such a lovely man who had touched so many in life and clearly many who had passed over before him too.

Sometimes people write and tell me about their near-death experiences. They report having been greeted by deceased relatives, angels, guides, old family friends, pets and old friends they didn't even know had died (these deaths being verified later, after they are resuscitated). If proof were still needed, these experiences providing previously unknown information must surely be enough.

Heavenly Healing

According to Debbie's dream visit, Dad appears to have 'woken up' on heaven-side. What happened in the intervening time? Dad may well have been through a period of healing before becoming aware of his death-state. This 'time' is not a reflection of time on our side of life as he seemed to begin communicating with us on 'this side' almost immediately. (The alarm clock went off 'on its own', music was played and manipulated, and mobiles started ringing and so on). To us, there seemed no 'gap of time' between him dying and reaching out to us.

Dr Michael Newton's book *Destiny of Souls* describes how after a challenging life a soul can go into a 'slumber chamber' to rest. After the passing of our Auntie Marlene who'd suffered many illnesses, Dad indicated to us that she'd found herself initially in what he called a 'healing pod'. Dad took Debbie to this 'place' in a dream-visitation experience, and when Debbie asked how long Auntie Marlene might remain in the healing pod, Dad replied, 'As long as she likes.'

Several months later, Aunt Marlene visited Debbie personally in a dream visitation. She informed Debbie, 'I've had a long rest and feel much better now.' Our aunt 'rested' for several months, but it's possible that other souls might need many Earth years' worth of restorative care in heaven. This might explain why some spirits are unable to visit loved ones on this side of life after they pass.

Other spirits go through a type of 'healing shower' after

death (I use this type of visualisation in my meditations and at workshops). Energy is pulsed through the soul 'body' in a type of therapeutic session or healing treatment.

As for what spirits do on the other side, during one dream Dad showed me that he was now working. Heaven offers many choices of career, based upon your soul growth. Dad showed me that he was helping to 'cross over' babies who'd passed on, guiding their souls to where they had to go in heaven. And our aunt told my sister that she had begun working with women who'd been unfortunate enough to die during childbirth. This was her heavenly role now – carer to Mums who'd died.

In his books, Dr Michael Newton lists a whole range of heavenly jobs including trainee spiritual guides, spiritual teachers and 'builders' of energy. Maybe there are as many careers in heaven as there are on Earth?

Jacky and Madeline: In our experience, we know that not everyone can have the contact that we have described, for reasons that aren't always clear.

It may be that the way in which we sleep is not conducive to after-life contact, possibly too deeply or too shallowly for example, but we do know that spirits will sometimes try and pass a message through friends or family members, especially young children, who seem more able to receive communication. It could also be that the spirits themselves are inexperienced or unenlightened as to the possibilities that are available to them. Perhaps they are simply occupied elsewhere.

A Promise Kept

In our case, Dad made a promise to his eldest daughter before he died that he'd visit from heaven, and even help her to write a book. He has certainly kept that promise. Like his brother Eric before him, he was determined to visit his loved ones on this side of life, and has seemed unwavering in his aim to prove life after death. We feel it likely that his many visits *are* the book he meant; the story of his life ... and afterlife. One visit is interesting. Two are fascinating. But after forty or more visits, and to a range of different people, even the most hardened sceptic must surely wonder if there might just be something in it, after all.

Everything Dad did *well* in life, everything that he was *known* for, he has showed us in death. His messages have illustrated that when his physical body was no longer able to do the things he loved, his spirit body, his soul, could continue with them. Dad's visitations have not been a random series of events. Each has been carefully planned, well thought out and brilliantly executed.

He enjoyed watching a movie ... and then fishing with Kyle. He was down at the riverbank for his grandsons first match; he danced with Madeline; he drove his car with Dianne, and when Debbie was distressed he hugged her. He cared for his wife when she worried about money and again when she was ill in hospital by warning Jacky in advance. He told his family to dry their tears, and showed them he was now surrounded by his loving family on the 'other side' of life ... as well as his many dogs!

Dad even shared little glimpses of future events. He was aware that Charlotte would pass her driving test and that we'd be overwhelmed with sympathy cards; and even further ahead in time, appearing at his granddaughters future wedding. He consoled his daughter Debbie by letting her know he was taking care of the granddaughter that never made it to *this side* of life. His life was carrying on ... just in a much better 'body'. He appeared young, fit and healthy, even *skipping* to prove his point! And now finally he'd managed to reach-out to his wife of over 53 years. They say, love conquers all – even death, and *they're* right!

Our experiences have been inspirational, moving and enormously valuable to us, during one of the saddest and most painful of experiences – the death of a dear and cherished loved one. Knowing that Dad is safe and well even though we can't be with him is extremely comforting, and has made our grieving process very different from how it might have been. Of course, we've cried and will no doubt continue to do so from time to time, and we still miss him from this side of life. But we feel the best way to honour his memory now is to live life to the fullest every single day.

Over to You

Our research has led us to the discovery that after-death communication is not just something that happens to a few people. To experience afterlife contact, even if it's just a sense that a lost one is sitting with you for a brief moment, is very common.

If you've lost a loved one, you too will have gone through the extreme physical pain of death. But to hope – to know – that life goes on, even in a form that you may not totally understand, can make death more bearable. To know your loved ones are safe, even if you can't be with them, brings great comfort. As time has passed, and maybe because more information is available, so that more people are now prepared to accept the signs for what they are, afterlife contact is becoming more and more common.

And you may experience it too – be it a touch, a smell, a voice or a dream visit.

We hope that reading this book has helped you to recall visitations and paranormal phenomena which previously you had written off merely as 'strange dreams' or 'weird' moments, and to discover that, after all, your loved ones have been there all along.

If you are still waiting for contact, we hope you have found our story of great comfort and that it has helped you to remain open. Ask for a sign – you can be specific – and then remember to acknowledge and accept it as 'truth' when you're given your signal. One of Jacky's requests was for a blue tit to come up to the window and this happened exactly as she had requested. Many people will ask for a white feather as a sign that their loved ones are around and they appear in unusual and unlikely places.

Stay open to the possibilities in your life, they are endless. You might read a message on a bill-board or a car number plate; maybe you'll catch an important song on the radio as we did, or tune-in to an appropriate television show. Sometimes we are drawn to a book cover, or the book will literally fall to the floor at your feet. Your own signs may be uniquely personal to you, so make a written note of your small coincidences so you can examine them closely at a later time. We wish you good luck.

If you want to share your afterlife experiences, you are welcome to contact Jacky, and if you would like some guidance on life-after-death please contact Madeline; our details are at the end of the book.

We firmly believe in life after death, and with so many experiences, many of them recorded here, we feel certain that this is not the end of Dad's story.

Because death *is* just the beginning . . .

RONALD GERALD HILL

Our father was a very special man to his family and his many friends. He lived a full and active life. His kind and gentle manner moved people everywhere he went. When he died, he left a big gap in our lives, and in the lives of the many people who'd known him. As one of our condolence cards read: 'A gentleman walked this way.'

*

CDs/DVDs by Jacky Newcomb

- *Healing with your Guardian Angel*, 2005; in this CD, Jacky uses the 'healing shower of light' mentioned on p. 218
- *Meet Your Guardian Angel*, 2005, Paradise Music
- *Angel Workshop*, 2006, Paradise Music
- *Ghosthunting Workshop*, Jacky Newcomb and Barrie John, 2010, Paradise Music
- *Angels* – a DVD presented by Jacky Newcomb and Shirley Crichton, 2005, New World Music

Author Websites

- Jacky Newcomb Media Site: **www.JackyNewcomb.com**
- Jacky's site about psychic children: **www.thepsychicchildren.com**
- Jacky's fan site: **www.AngelLady.co.uk**
- Madeline Richardson: **www.MadelineRichardson.co.uk**

Resources

In writing this book, we have referred to and enjoyed many books and websites on related subjects. Here is a list of some of our favourites:

Books

- *The Vortex: Key to Future Science*, David Ash and Peter Hewitt, Salamander Books, 1995
- *Between Death and Life: Conversations With a Spirit*, Dolores Cannon, Gateway, 2003
- *Living Magically*, Gill Edwards, Piatkus, 1991

- *Journeys Through Time: A Guide to Reincarnation and Your Immortal Soul*, Soozi Holbeche, Piatkus Books, 1996
- *Out on a Limb*, Shirley MacLaine, Bantam Books, 1986
- *Journey of Souls: Case Studies of Life Between Lives*, Dr Michael Newton, PhD, Llewellyn Worldwide, 1994
- *Destiny of Souls: New Case Studies of Life Between Lives*, Dr Michael Newton, PhD, Llewellyn Worldwide, 2000
- *The Unbelievable Truth: A Medium's Guide to the Spirit World*, Gordon Smith, Hay House, 2005
- *A Lawyer Presents the Case for the Afterlife*, Victor J. Zammit, Krylov, 2007

Websites

- www.victorzammit.com – website of renowned afterlife expert
- www.whatthebleep.com – *What the Bleep do we know!?*, film/book about quantum physics, spirituality, neurology and evolution thought
- www.hagelin.org – website of the world-renowned quantum physicist John Hagelin
- www.robertlanza.com – website of one of the leading scientists in the world and author of hundreds of publications
- www.ramtha.com – Ramtha's School of Enlightenment, for the teachings of 'Ramtha', mystic, philosopher and master teacher, channelled by J. Z. Knight
- www.astraldynamics.com – website of Robert Bruce, author and out-of-body-experience expert
- www.monroeinstitute.org – website of the Monroe Institute

which provides experiential education programmes that facilitate the personal exploration of human consciousness

- www.newtoninstitute.org – website of the Newton Institute, founded by Michael Newton, PhD, who holds a doctorate in counselling psychology, is an author and master hypnotherapist

- www.iands.org – International Association for Near-death Studies

- www.near-death.com – Near-death Experiences and the Afterlife website

- www.iacworld.org – International Academy of Consciousness website

About the authors

Jacky Newcomb

Jacky is a presenter and *Sunday Times* bestselling author. She has published twelve books on paranormal themes, including many relating specifically to afterlife contact. Jacky has won the SCA award for Most Popular Author/Book in both 2007 and 2008 and, more recently, the *Soul & Spirit* magazine Favourite Angel Expert and Favourite Spiritual Author readers' choice awards in 2009, as well as the silver award in 2010.

Jacky is regularly interviewed in the national press about her expertise in angels, afterlife and other paranormal experiences. She has been featured in the *Daily Mail*, *Daily Express*, *News of the World* and many newspapers, as well as appearing as a regular guest on radio shows around the world.

Jacky has been a guest-expert several times on *This Morning* and also *LK Today*, *Psychic Live* and other shows. She is a columnist for *Fate & Fortune* magazine and has published many hundreds of articles on paranormal subjects. She has several celebrity clients. She is known for her easygoing, 'chatty' style

of writing and is celebrated for the way she brings the 'normal' back into the paranormal world.

Jacky now lives in Cornwall with her husband of over twenty-five years and her two cats. She is a proud mother and nana.

Contact Jacky

Jacky welcomes readers' paranormal stories. You can contact her through her publishers or email via her website. For more information about Jacky Newcomb, her books and her work, visit www.JackyNewcomb.com (media) or www.AngelLady.co.uk (fan site). Jacky is also on Facebook and Twitter.

Madeline Richardson

Writer and paranormal researcher, Madeline Richardson has been studying paranormal phenomena for over twenty years. She has provided psychic research for many published features for magazines and e-zines.

Madeline has investigated numerous instances of past-life regression and has had frequent experiences of her own. Her captivating studies have taken her from an irrefutable belief in the afterlife to quantum physics and parallel universes, researching the science behind the mysteries. She has studied such diverse subjects as crop circles, ancient and sacred sites, hypnosis and regression analysis, esoteric lore, mysticism and metaphysics. She is an expert on afterlife communication.

Madeline lives in Cornwall. As well as her writing and research, Madeline works as a Guidance Officer. She holds an NVQ in Advice and Guidance, a Professional Certificate of Merit in Counselling, and is a CCC-registered counsellor.

Contact Madeline

Madeline welcomes readers' afterlife queries. You can contact her through her publishers or email via her website. For more information about Madeline Richardson, visit www.MadelineRichardson.co.uk. Madeline is also on Facebook.

Madeline and Jacky are sisters ... and friends
Call Me When You Get to Heaven is their first book together.

Further reading and resources

The dead don't die. They look on and help.

D. H. Lawrence

Other Books by Jacky Newcomb

- *An Angel Treasury*, Harper Element, 2004
- *Little Angel Love*, Harper Element, 2005
- *An Angel Saved My Life*, Harper Element, 2006
- *An Angel By My Side*, Harper Element, 2006
- *An Angel Held My Hand*, Harper Element, 2007
- *Angels Watching Over Me*, Hay House, 2007
- *A Faerie Treasury*, Hay House, 2007
- *Angel Kids*, Hay House, 2008
- *Dear Angel Lady*, Hay House, 2009
- *Angel Secrets*, Godsfield Press, 2010
- *I Can See Angels*, Hay House, 2010
- *Healed by an Angel*, Hay House, 2011